Afro-Irish Links:
A Shared Cultural History

Also written by Slough West Indian Peoples Enterprise

Remember The Times (2014)

Afro-Irish Links:
A Shared Cultural History

Slough West Indian Peoples Enterprise

Researched by Jenny Callaghan, Michael Callaghan, Paul Crooks, Frank Doherty, Jamie Green & Robert Martin Kelly

Edited by Robert Martin Kelly

SWIPE
2019

Afro-Irish Links: A Shared Cultural History

First Printing: 2019

ISBN 978-0-244-53174-4

Slough West Indian Peoples Enterprise
The Jubilee River Riverside Centre
Slough Rd, Slough SL1 2BP

www.swipemusic.com

Contents

Slaves working on a plantation (illustration by Edmund Oliver, 1877)

Acknowledgements

Thanks to Heritage Lottery Funding, Blackkactus, The Blarney Pilgrims, Bullseye Awards, Creative Academy, Clayton Hodge, Serena Kelly, George Kirkham, Pastor George Koroma from Sierra Leone, Natalie Mania, Yvonne Mania, Charmaine Niles, Joy Okpighe, Charlie Palmer, the pastors and congregation of Shiloah Church, Slough Irish Club, Renae Sylvan, Yvette Sylvan, The Reverend Cadman White from Montserrat, Charlotte Williams.

Foreword

The town of Slough in the United Kingdom is a multicultural area with a significant population of Caribbean and second generation Irish citizens. I had noticed that there were many people in both communities that had the same surnames, and after some initial research found that there was evidence going back to the seventeenth century of African and Irish people working side by side on the plantations in the Caribbean - the beginning of a cultural fusion.

The angle that particularly interested me was the impact this cultural fusion had on the development of music in the Caribbean and in particular, Jamaica. At the outset of this research project, I felt that it was important to get the views of academics and other subject matter experts who could provide insight into the development of Jamaican and Caribbean music between the seventeenth century and present date, describe how Europeans and Africans came together to develop this music, and give a balanced view of the historical significance of what took place. This book not only documents those views but also serves to document the experiences of Caribbean and Irish people in Slough so future generations can understand the experiences of their forefathers.

I would like to take this opportunity to say a big thank you to members of the Caribbean and Irish communities in Slough who took part in the project, and also to the academics who gave up their valuable time to participate and give us the benefit of their expertise and lastly, a big thanks to the Heritage Lottery and the players, without whose help the project would not be possible.

Hilton Callaghan

Preface

In the course of this project a number of academics were interviewed in order to understand the roots of the African and Irish cultures that came to the Caribbean in the seventeenth century. This was the era of slavery when Africans were transported as slaves to work on the plantations.

A history that is less well known is that of the Irish, who were shipped to the Caribbean as prisoners of war as a result of the Cromwellian conquest of Ireland from 1649-1653. Others came voluntarily, working as indentured servants, offering their labour for a fixed period in exchange for promises of plots of land when the term was completed. Among the planter class were a number of Irish merchants who sought profit and wealth from the region.

This project looked at the evidence that the academics discussed in order to understand the context of Caribbean society that was undergoing an influx of disparate peoples from two different parts of the world. But within these cultures music and dance was integral to their political power, history, celebrations and rituals.

From the era of slavery, through the Americas, up to immigration in the present day - when Afro-Caribbean and Irish people came to the UK in the 1950s-1960s bringing their music and culture with them – we can see that music and dance offered hope to displaced people and those who found themselves in an unfamiliar land. The styles that emerged into the twentieth century were based on the vernacular musical traditions, folk music that spoke of the lives of ordinary people. It is a testimony to the worldwide appeal of the musical styles that came later that they speak a universal language to those seeking new forms of community.

For the second part of this project we interviewed people in Slough who came from the Caribbean and Ireland. They talked about the music and culture they brought with them - that not only helped maintain their bonds with their countrymen - but that appealed to and enriched the society into which they had come to.

Introduction

Jamaican people living in Britain have some appreciation of Jamaica's Irish heritage. Some will know of Jamaican towns with names such as Irish Town, Dublin Castle, Caramel, Kildare, Belfast and Middleton. Others answer to Irish surnames passed down through generations; names such as: Collins, O'Hare, McCormick, McCarthy, Burke, Clarke, O'Callaghan, McKay and O'Connor.

Barbadians also answer to Irish surnames. Some speak of communities of people living in Barbados of Irish descent.

The flag of Montserrat is adorned with Erin, female personification of Ireland, playing the golden harp.

Then there are others, younger people of both Caribbean and Irish descent, living in Britain, who have little or no knowledge of a Caribbean and Irish heritage that was once shared.

This booklet provides some insight into what is an intriguing topic. It describes how two apparently disparate cultures, African and Irish, blended through music and dance. It also describes how they influenced the development of Caribbean music culture down through the generations.

The booklet is published with a view to giving the Caribbean and Irish communities in Britain deeper and mutual appreciation of a shared, but not often spoken about, heritage.

"When an old man dies, a library burns to the ground."

African Proverb

"If you're lucky enough to be Irish, you're lucky enough."

Irish Proverb

1

Interviews With Academics

SWIPE is grateful to the following academics, who we interviewed in 2019 and who contributed to this project. With the information they provided we were able to direct our research into the topics covered in this book.

Ellen Campbell-Grizzle is a lecturer, formally the Dean at the University of Technology in Jamaica where she now teaches Caribbean Pharmacy History. She is by profession a social pharmacist, focusing on non-clinical areas, specialising in health communication.

Laurent Dubois is a professor at Duke University in Durham, North Carolina, USA. He works on the history and culture of the Caribbean. He is the author of "The Banjo: America's African instrument".

Sir Howard Fergus KBE is a Montserratian author and historian. He is a former professor at the University of the West Indies and is interested in the history of the Caribbean and Montserrat. He is also an established poet.

Eamonn Galldubh is a musician (uilleann piper and flautist) and researcher from Dublin. He is carrying out research from Dundalk Institute of Technology and his research interest is on the history of Irish music.

Nicole Jacoberger is an assistant professor of history at Camden County College in New Jersey, USA. She is an Atlantic World historian specialising in the seventeenth to nineteenth century Irish Caribbean.

Mary Caton Lingold is a professor of English at Virginia Commonwealth University, USA. She is also a musician and her research focuses on Sonic Life and Musical Production in the African Atlantic world. As well as Sound Studies and Digital Humanities, her research specialisation in terms of literature is in the colonial

Americas: colonial travel writing about the Caribbean, the Atlantic world and descriptions of plantation slavery.

Meleisa Ono-George is an associate professor of Caribbean history based at the University of Warwick.

PART 1: A SHARED MUSICAL HERITAGE

"A people without the knowledge of their past history, origin and culture is like a tree without roots."

Marcus Garvey

"Slaves are generally expected to sing as well as to work."

Frederick Douglass

"Just give me your hand,
Tabhair dom do lámh.
Just give me your hand,
For the world it is ours.
All the sea and the land,
To destroy or command,
If you give me your hand.
Just give me your hand,
In a gesture of peace.
Will you give me your hand
And all troubles will cease,
For the strong and the weak,
For the rich and the poor?
All peoples and creeds,
Let's meet their needs.
With a passion, we can fashion,
A new world of love."

Ruaidri Dáll Ó Catháin (*Tabhair dom do Lámh*, 1603)

Humankind's Music Heritage

Early life is where the seeds are planted and grow into our values, beliefs and attitudes. Early life is where we experience music as part of the family unit. As we go through life, we develop our inborn musicality. We listen, dance, sing and play instruments. Musical experiences are so important to helping us construct meaning and understanding of ourselves, our culture and our world.

As we mature, we become exposed to the range of musical influences that bring into focus aspects of differences in ethnicity, social class, geographical region, religion, musical structure, age and gender. On one level, the meanings we apply to music come from personal associations with it. We derive meaning from our abilities to perceive and organize relationships of musical sounds. On another level, the meaning we attribute to music is shaped by our social, historical, cultural and political environment.

Nearly all of us are born with the potential to make music. Our inborn ability to develop that potential is ultimately influenced by life experiences within cultural circles.

History can recall how music was instrumental in changing and shaping social order and social realities within the islands of the Caribbean. There, popular culture is primarily oral rather than written. Caribbean music culture grew as a result of many musical influences and experiences. It is a part of the world where music has traditionally been transmitted through physical contact with other people. Indeed, when Irish people and Africans came into social contact within the Caribbean, it was music culture that played an important role in binding these disparate people together.

Music And Society In Ireland In The Seventeenth Century

Music was integral to Irish society, in 1674 the English writer Richard Head wrote about Ireland "in every field a fiddle, and the lasses footing it till they were all of a foam" to reference to ubiquity of music in Irish life. Tied in with wakes, holidays, weddings and informal gatherings music would have been experienced in many different contexts in society.

A royal clerk to the king and two archbishops, Gerald of Wales (Giraldus Cambrensis) wrote his work *Topographia Hibernica* ("Topography of Ireland") in 1187. In a passage that refers to Ireland he states: "The only thing to which I find that this people apply a commendable industry is playing upon musical instruments; in which they are incomparably more skillful than any other nation I have ever seen". As Eamonn Galldubh (interview 2019) highlighted on the one hand this is a compliment but with a sting within it.

Gerald's writings depict Ireland and Irish in very unfavourable terms but he continued this passage noting the musical ability of the Irish musicians: "For their modulation on these instruments, unlike that of the Britons to which I am accustomed, is not slow and harsh, but lively and rapid, while the harmony is both sweet and gay. It is astonishing that in so complex and rapid a movement of the fingers, the musical proportions can be preserved."

The Brehon Laws of the eighth and ninth centuries codified everyday life. There are particular laws that illustrate the high status of harpists, for example severe penalties are decreed for any person who borrows a tuning key and does not return it in a timely manner. The inscription of harps on stone crosses further confirms the venerated position these musicians had in Irish society.

The seventeenth century was a turbulent period for Ireland, The Battle of Kinsale saw the English conquest of Gaelic Ireland in 1602. The "Flight of the Earls" followed when Hugh O'Neill, Earl of Tyrone and leader of the Irish resistance, left for Spain with his supporters and other chieftains. Territories left behind were seized by

Presbyterian Lowland Scots and northern English settlers as the Plantation of Ulster commenced. Following the Irish Rebellion of 1641, most of Ireland came under the control of the Irish Catholic Confederation, formed by Irish Catholic nobles, clergy and military leaders. But the wars waged by Oliver Cromwell completed the British colonisation of Ireland.

A bard with a harp (bottom right) playing for members of the court. From *The Image of Irelande* (1581) by John Derrick.

The repercussions were felt by Ireland as the old bardic traditions were devastated when the Gaelic aristocracy fled. The harpists had enjoyed a powerful social status under the Irish chieftains, they were the oral historians giving them political influence akin to the spin doctors of the present day. As the Gaelic elite left Ireland they were forced to seek patronage from other sources, playing to the peasantry rather than the aristocracy. Many sought refuge in Scotland or among the Anglo-Irish ascendancy.

One of the most notable harpists and composers of the period was Ruaidri Dáll Ó Catháin who was a gentleman by birth, his family were hereditary allies of the O'Neill dynasty. His most famous composition is a 1603 piece called *Tabhair dom do Lámh* (*Give Me Your Hand*) which is still performed at weddings today in Ireland. Captain Francis O'Neill, collector of Irish traditional music, told the story of how the song was written that illustrates the high social status of harpists: "proud and spirited, he resented anything in the nature of trespass on his dignity. Among his visits to the houses of Scottish nobility, he is said to have called at Eglinton Castle, Ayrshire. Knowing he was a harper, but being unaware of his rank, Lady Eglinton commanded him to play a tune. Taking offence at her peremptory manner, Ó Catháin refused and left the castle. When she found out who her guest was her ladyship sought and effected a speedy reconciliation".

Ó Catháin finished his life in Scotland, as did William and Thomas Connellan who wrote some of the oldest surviving tunes *Molly MacAlpin* and *Molly St. George* in the seventeenth century. Those who moved to Scotland escaped the political events that displaced many in Irish society. On Cromwell's orders around 500 harps were burned in Dublin. The English were concerned about the position of the harp and targeted harpists, it was not just a musical instrument but a tool that could be used to incite political and historical views. The musician Edward Bunting was the first to systematically collect Irish music, by the time he organised the Belfast Harp Festival in 1792 only a handful of harps could be found.

A lot of the musical pieces from this time are laments, often marches that referred to the battles and the huge loss of life. In addition to 15,000 – 20,000 battlefield casualties during the Cromwellian conquests, 200,000 – 600,000 civilians died as a result of violence, famine or disease. A further 12,000 were deported to the Americas as indentured labourers. When one considers the population of Ireland was at this time 1.2 million, this illustrates that a huge proportion of Irish people would have experienced the consequences of this campaign.

As well as the harp, a number of other musical instruments were played in Ireland during this period. The fiddle, as mentioned in Richard Head's quote, was an adaptation of the Italian instrument. There are very few surviving examples of the bagpipes what were played. They were based on an ancient version of this instrument, similar to the Scottish pipes; the uilleann pipes were not developed until the eighteenth century. The less wealthy in Ireland played a version of the jaws harp.

Most of the surviving examples of this music are in collections located outside of Ireland. A late sixteenth century piece in a London private collection is titled *Irish March*. In the seventeenth century more often dance pieces were recorded, in the Playford collections there are pieces of music for dancing. Some of these reference the country but do not sound Irish. It was not until the eighteenth century that the transcriptions became more rigorous when musicians such as Bunting started their collections. The hornpipes, reels and jigs that are associated with Ireland today are not the same as in the seventeenth century.

Of the harp pieces, the largest body of work comes from Turlough O'Carolan (1670-1738), many of his works have titles attributed to his patrons. Ruaidri Dáll Ó Catháin is cited as the possible writer of the melody *Derry Air*, the words were added in 1910 and the song became *Danny Boy*, with lyrics that reference the Irish diaspora. Pieces composed by the Connellan brothers are sometimes played today as are the Marches - music for the noble families the O'Donnell's, O'Neill's and O'Sullivan's.

Music And Society In Africa In The Seventeenth Century

The vast majority of slaves came from West Africa and they came from many diverse societies. Their religious practices were unique and varying. They therefore had no unifying language, religion, or musical tradition. Pre-colonial maps do not match those of the present, but even within today's borders the captured people came from the ethnical diverse nations of Ghana, Benin, Gambia, the Democratic Republic of Congo, Nigeria, Senegal, Angola and countries in the West African region. Slaves were also sourced from Eastern Africa and as far as Madagascar, but fewer came from these regions.

Among the later waves brought to the Caribbean were Yorouba speaking populations from West Africa, whose religion included the worship of divine beings that would possess spirits and speak through them. These religions have persisted throughout the Caribbean, under various names and using various musical forms. Called Obeah in Jamaica and other names in other countries, they usually employ a set of three sacred drums and other instruments whose rhythms are specific to divine beings. Called by the rhythms, the gods descend and "ride" the bodies of specific worshippers. Though formerly persecuted in some countries, these religions have been expanded to new audiences.

Within these societies there did exist significant similarities and familiarities, as well as differences. In the Senegal/Gambia area a number of ethnic groups existed, for example the Wolof, Mandinka and the Fula peoples. These groups are distinctive but would have interacted and been familiar with each another, they may have known each other's languages. As a result of the European powers colonising the continent, there were also Portuguese and French speaking Africans and Islamic migration also occurred in the area. So the West of Africa was an incredibly diverse region, more so with the existence of the slave trading ports that saw large numbers of people coming and going.

As with Ireland, music within West African the societies was extremely important. At the very top of the social pyramid, in the court music setting a king had a band of musicians who preceded him in formal processions, a tradition comparable to European monarch traditions of the day. European travelers commented on this similarity, trumpets, horns (usually made from ivory rather than brass) and drums were often used – even the instrument styles were familiar. Informal vernacular music was just as vital, playing a role in religious ritual settings.

Africans brought general musical traits that transcended particular African Communities - among them the collective approach to making music featuring call and response singing, and dense and often interlocking rhythms played on drums. Well suited to communal performance in general, call and-response is often infused with narrative text, responsorial singing, or a drum solo and many types of African Caribbean music. The most notable features of African music include its emphasis on rhythm.

Manuel, Bilby and Largey (1995) describe the African sound as "rich in melody, timbral variety, and even two and three-part harmony, but if there is often the most important aesthetic parameter, distinguishing songs and genres and commanding the focus of the performers and listeners attention. Accordingly, the leaders of African and African Caribbean traditional music are often formidably complex in ways that lack any counterparts in western folk or common-practice classical music. Much of the interest and complexity derives from the interaction of regular pulses (whether silent or audible) and off beat accents. This feature is often described as 'syncopation'".

Dance also had an expression in all these settings - informal, vernacular, celebratory or religious. Traditions existed whereby people within families were trained to perform in court and performed various social roles. The Griots were members of a caste of people served as historians, storytellers, praise singers, poets or musicians. As Francis Bebey (1969) states: "The West African griot is a troubadour, the counterpart of the medieval European minstrel... The griot knows everything that is going on... He is a living archive of the people's traditions... The virtuoso talents of the griots command universal admiration. This virtuosity is the culmination of long years of study and hard work under the tuition of a teacher who is often a father or uncle. The profession is by no means a male prerogative. There are many women griots whose talents as singers and musicians are equally remarkable."

An African Griot

Griots were historians, storytellers, praise singers, poets or musicians. They were a repository of oral tradition, their role equivalent to the bards found in British and Gaelic cultures.

As in Europe, in terms of musical traditions there were broad similarities between societies, some instruments crossed boundaries but playing styles could be different. The bala or balafon for example: sometimes they were played standing, they could be worn over shoulders or played free standing, some had gourd resonators, others played them seated with no resonator. There was a variation in the style instruments were played according to the society and its setting.

The Irish Arrival To The Caribbean

The arrival of Europeans in the Caribbean brought about irreversible demographic change. The Spanish and Portuguese arrived first, bringing new diseases and defeat for the indigenous inhabitants, decimating the population in the space of only a few decades. The British, Scottish and Irish arrived in the Caribbean not long after, slipping into more neglected Spanish possessions in the Eastern Caribbean. Africans stolen from Africa and the high proportion Irish people ejected from Ireland were thrown together, within the British Caribbean during the seventeenth, eighteenth and nineteenth centuries.

From the 1620s, official accounts record the arrival of Irish labourers in the Caribbean, there were reports that some of them were kidnapped by press-gangs operating in the areas of the principal ports in Munster. The journey took almost three months, and those who survived the Atlantic crossing found conditions on the plantations extremely harsh. They worked as indentured servants for a fixed period of time, "under a yoke harsher than that of the Turks", before eventually obtaining their freedom. After seven years of service, some did acquire small landholdings, but there is no evidence to document any returned to Ireland.

Most of the Irish labour arrived following the Cromwellian conquest from 1649-1653. During the English Civil War the Irish Catholic Confederation (formed by Irish Catholic nobles, clergy and military leaders after the Irish Rebellion of 1641) allied themselves with the English Royalists who intended to restore the monarchy. This posed a major threat to Cromwell's regime and his New Model Army was dispatched to crush the Catholic power.

Following the siege of Drogheda in 1649 and the massacre of the garrison Cromwell stated: "When they submitted, their officers were knocked on the head, and every tenth man of the soldiers killed, and the rest shipped for the Barbadoes". The war in Ireland was particularly brutal, though such conduct was not unusual in this historical period. Many Parliamentarians wished to punish the Irish for atrocities committed against English Protestant settlers during the

1641 Uprising and Cromwell's New Model Army were predominantly Puritan who considered the war a crusade against Roman Catholic heretics.

Cromwell's secretary of state John Thurloe wrote in his *State Papers*, that it was "a measure beneficial to Ireland, which was thus relieved of a population that might trouble the planters, and of great benefit to the sugar planters who desired the men and boys for their bondsmen and women and Irish girls in a country where they had only Maroon women and Negresses to solace them". Cromwell's son, Henry was made Major General in command of the forces in Ireland and it was under his reign that hundreds of thousands of Irish men and women were shipped to the West Indies.

Cromwell passed a series of Penal Laws against Roman Catholics (the vast majority of the population), those who participated in the Irish Catholic Confederation had all their land confiscated. From 1648 - 1655 around 12,000 Irish political prisoners were shipped to Barbados. Although indentured servants (Irish included) had been coming to Barbados since 1627, this new wave of arrivals were the first to come involuntarily. The Irish prisoners made up for a serious labour shortage caused by English planters' lack of access to African slaves. The Dutch and Portuguese dominated the slave trade in the early seventeenth century and most white land owners in Barbados and the neighbouring islands were unable to purchase African slaves. By the late seventeenth century the Irish comprised a substantial portion of certain Caribbean colony populations.

A Jesuit priest, Father J.J. Williams, in his 1932 book *The Black Irish of Jamaica* details the subsequent shipments from Barbados and direct from "The Auld Sod". The last shipment appears to have been in 1841 from Limerick, aboard the SS Robert Kerr, a voyage that took seven weeks. The Kingston Gleaner newspaper noted that "they landed in Kingston wearing their best clothes and temperance medals", the temperance medals signifying that they did not drink alcohol.

Barbados, which received the majority of deportees from Ireland, still has a small population of "red shanks" or "red legs" – descendants of the Irish indentured labourers, much the same as Jamaicans of German ancestry in Seaford Town in St. James. St. Kitts was another destination where the labourers ended up.

Due to their intransient nature they were abused as indentured labourers. Typically they were hired for up to seven years, but planters worked them as much as they could. Richard Ligon documented servant abuse in his two years in Barbados, his 1657 work *A True and Exact History of the Island of Barbadoes* described planters beating servants with canes if they were deemed lethargic or if they complained about working conditions. He also wrote that indenture time was doubled for servants who resisted. In the same year the Barbados Council decreed that free men, women and servants of the Irish nation who wondered as vagabonds refusing to labour should be whipped according to the law. A decade later English adventurer John Scott described these servants as Irish poor men who are just permitted to live branded with the epithet of "white slaves".

At this stage it is important to emphasise that Irish labourers in the Caribbean were indentured servants, they were not slaves. Indentured servitude was a form of temporary bondage and their status was unfree, but to call the Irish "slaves" infers that they had the same status as African chattel slaves, who were categorised as the property of their masters in the same way as livestock. Chattel slavery was perpetual and it was permissible to punish African slaves through torture, mutilation and death. The Irish were persons in law; Africans were property named along with cattle and livestock, given a monetary value rather than a name.

Indentured servants were afforded the same rights as servants working in Europe. Court documents record that abuses did occur – in 1640 a servant in Barbados called John Thomas was tortured by his master and sought legal redress, he was compensated for his treatment and his masters imprisoned. Laws passed in the 1640-1660 period specified the legal distinctions between slavery (as reserved for "Negroes") and servitude (as reserved for Europeans).

While on Barbados many of the Irish were indentured labourers, over on the island of Montserrat the Irish population included people from all social classes from indentured servant to governor, which illustrates they represented both the colonised and the colonisers. Likewise in Jamaica some ten per cent of the property owners in 1670 were Irish. Merchant families from towns like Waterford and Galway earned great wealth through trading networks with the Caribbean. Court ledgers and private papers of the Irish planter class reveal they were often enthusiastic exploiters of the African slave trade, their laws and court records emphasise distinctions between the status and treatment of indentured servants (also usually Irish) and chattel slaves.

Indentured labourers believed they would return home following their term of work, but letters and documents from the time show there were efforts by the authorities to prevent this. The labourers were from the lowest classes in society and simply did not have the financial means to return, too many factors were against them.

By the 1640s, a preference for using enslaved African labour was emerging. However, Irish servants considerably outnumbered the black population in the Caribbean. The Barbados Assembly tried by legislative action to restrict the increase in Irish Catholics in the colony. By 1660 some twenty per cent of the servant population was Irish. It is estimated in the years immediately following 1660, 10,000 settlers, mostly servants, frustrated by their inability to gain access to land, left the island. Half of them left for Jamaica, the other half left for mainland America, the Leeward Islands, Windward Islands and Surinam.

By 1667 Lord Willoughby, a visiting British governor, described Montserrat as "almost an Irish colony". A census taken a decade later showed that almost seventy per cent of the white population were Irish (male and female). On Nevis and Antigua, the Irish totaled around twenty-five per cent white population; on St. Christopher they hovered around ten per cent. Earlier attempts to restrict the flow of Irish were ineffective, and the British were demonstrably unenthusiastic about the possibility of an official Irish colony in the Caribbean.

Because of the abuses endured by indentured servants it led to a lot of runaways and rebellions, with those deemed riotous and unruly relocated to Montserrat. Nicole Jacoberger (interview 2019) noted that this happened in 1632 with St. Kitts and in 1643 with Barbados. Montserrat saw a slowly growing population of Irish with an African slave population on the island. Collusion between the two groups did happen and this worried the authorities, laws were enacted to prevent this. This is how we know they were working alongside each other and were somehow cooperating with each other. The difference between the Irish and Africans was in their punishment: for the indentured labourers this was often extension of their term or they were fined in sugar. The Africans were punished brutally - tortured, mutilated or murdered for running away.

The Irish were given more rights in the long run. Their status was defined in terms of religion - Catholics were typically the labourers, Protestants typically the wealthy planter class. The status of Irish Catholics changed due to fears over rebellion and loss of the colony. England assured of white coherence and loyalty by allowing the advancement of some Irish Catholics who prioritised loyalty over religion. The earliest example was the appointment of William Stapleton as Montserrat's first Irish Catholic governor in 1668. He was rewarded for his loyalty to The Crown during the French takeover of the island in 1666 - 1667, while many Irish Protestants were not. Stapleton was an excellent record keeper with historians today benefitting from his census documents.

Montserrat's Irish population was afforded opportunities denied to them elsewhere, but this largely impacted a small echelon of society who controlled all the arable land. Many former servants fell into the poor white community of Montserrat, who worked alongside the black community. England continually tried to separate these groups by offering legal advantages to the white community in order to differentiate them from the black labouring communities. To help the white community sell its goods, in 1736 the Montserrat Assembly made it illegal for the black community to profit in the public markets by prohibiting them planting certain crops.

The Blake Brothers were Irish emigrants who settled in Barbados and Montserrat and made a fortune, they often wrote home to Galway espousing the good living that could be made in the new land. The Blake Estates that are still in place on Montserrat date back to the wealth the Blakes earned from the plantations.

While some Irish became part of the planter class and became wealthy, something they could not do in Ireland, others were vagrants, they wandered around and ended up in the poor white community unable to support themselves. As Nicole Jacoberger stated (interview 2019), the arable land went to a select few in the planter class; the average worker freed from indenture looking for land had a very hard time finding available plots, after the hard years of indenture this was very traumatic as they were unable to make a new life for themselves.

From the seventeenth century to the nineteenth century the Irish could be found at every level of white society and the Caribbean. They helped to turn the Caribbean into the world's sugar bowl. The lesser-known well known history of indentured servitude in the Caribbean would lay solid foundations for the transition to black slavery – the period when Africans became the most numerous group on the islands.

Music, Culture And Survival: African Slaves In The Caribbean

While Africans were transported to the Caribbean the social structures that bear culture could not be brought. People arrived as individuals, sometimes those with common language were kept together, but in most cases people found themselves among those from other societies and regions. The continent of Africa was an incredibly diverse space, people did not share language.

There is a spectrum of opinion on how culture developed in the Caribbean and the extent to which Africans brought over their culture or reconstituted what was in place. Music was a great connector, if language was not understood music could connect. Creole languages emerged across the Caribbean, formed from the contact of European languages (English, French, Spanish or Portuguese) with African languages spoken by the slaves. There was an African-European cultural fusion, but also an infra-African creolisation, a fusion so they could find a common language.

Slavers bringing captives on board a slave ship on Africa's west coast (image circa nineteenth century)

Under enslavement the formal purposes of shows of state were removed as the workers were subjugated. Europeans knew the Africans used trumpets and horns knowing they were associated with state pomp and also warfare, so they were outlawed as they were being used in uprisings.

Some who were brought over were musicians, if not they would have experienced music in other social settings. This gave rise to new cultural forms that were African-based, bringing them together in other ways. As an example of this, the banjo is based on an African instrument, but is a representation, not an exact replication of the lutes that were played in Africa.

Similarly with dance, forms were developed that spoke to a lot of different cultures in order to unite them. Laurent Dubois noted (interview 2019) that traditional styles were condensed and unified into a form that connected those who were displaced. Some Africans were located where they did have a similar background, language and culture, in those conditions certain dances were retained. An alternative view is that a new creolised culture was created – it depended on the demographics and the situation. Generally, people created a more inclusive culture that allowed African people to share, in most cases there was not enough density of people from one particular society to sustain a specific cultural life.

The experiences of those who were born in Africa, captured and trafficked to the Caribbean, was different from those born into plantation society. Enslaved survivors of the middle passage would strive to gather with people from their traditions and cultural heritage whenever they could, this is logical and to be expected of displaced peoples. However there were incredible demands on labour, time, health and attention; often slaves didn't have the mental, physical or material resources to recreate their traditions and make their music.

Sugar production was so hard on the body with so many succumbing to early death that a constant import of labour was needed. For centuries people were being imported, so there was a constant influx of African knowledge and tradition into slave society, especially into the Caribbean.

Jean-Baptiste Labat, more commonly called "Father Labat" – a missionary in the French Antilles – wrote extensively about dance in the seventeenth century. He described dances that brought together different traditions, but were not necessarily from one in particular. They became popular with the slaves and also with white society with startling speed. People needed music and dance to confront the hell of plantation slavery and to connect, forms of community and survival, to look back to a better past and a better future.

A popular genre of literature at this time was called travel writing that comes out of an ancient tradition of writing by adventurers, whether colonials, sailors or governors of colonies. They were sometimes motivated to write to impress monarchs and bankers to fund their enterprises. People also read them voraciously as they described the new worlds. It was a generic custom to document the ethnographic descriptions of the people encountered. Music was almost universally written about, in some descriptions the Europeans didn't like or understand what they heard.

There is very little evidence of the music that survived in this early period, however Laurent Dubois, Mary Caton Lingold (who SWIPE interviewed in 2019 for this project) along with David K. Garner have undertaken research on the earliest known record - it comes from the natural historian Hans Sloane who was from an Irish colonial family. Sloane studied plants and fauna and noted the indigenous Caribbean and slave people had great knowledge in this area. He also brought back some musical instruments to his collection, which have sadly been lost. Published in 1707 his book on the natural history of the islands *Voyage to the Islands of Madera, Barbados, Nieves, S. Christophers and Jamaica*, contains one single page on music from Jamaica with notation. There are five pieces of music *Angola*, *Papa* and three under the title *Koromanti*. Sloane recorded they were played at a festival where black musicians came together. The music was written down by someone named Mr. Baptiste, who is likely from African descent and must have had musical training. The document allows us to listen to pieces of improvisation and music from the time. On just that single page are pieces that are all extremely different music styles from various regions of Africa, exemplifying that people would experience different styles of music at a single gathering as early as the 1680s.

In Sloane's book there are images of lute-like instruments, they have a gourd with a skin and a neck. There are other accounts of balafon and marimba-style instruments and by eighteenth century the mbira, also known as thumb pianos. Added to this were various improvisations as people were making instruments from scratch.

In John Gabriel Stedman's work *The Narrative of a Five Years Expedition against the Revolted Negroes of Surinam* (1796) the musical notation is a little less faithfully reproduced, but in his narrative is an illustrated plate (from the years 1772–1777) of twenty eight instruments, he carefully described what they sounded like, how they were played and from which African tradition they come from. Stedman's document shows that even towards the end of the eighteen century African traditions were surviving even as creolisation was occurring.

Africans were also playing European instruments and significant numbers became trained in music and theatre traditions. In Saint-Domingue (Haiti) many of the orchestra members were slaves. Posters that listed runaway slaves provide a description of their skills and "musician" was common, most often playing the violin. It was a skill that a slave escaping to an urban area could use as a livelihood. In Saint-Domingue there were musicians who had a profession of playing for other slaves at gatherings.

They may even have been paid and had a stature, this is reflected in the fact that in records their names are stated, often their stage names. Having this talent afforded musicians a means to earn should they be emancipated. Slave musicians played at gatherings of whites, in orchestras and at private dwellings. In Virginia, USA at gatherings of planters, slaves played music such as Congo minuets, illustrating that though trained in European music they were able to bring elements of their own culture.

The people building instruments were in a completely different context from Africa and required to use different woods and materials. In the case of the banjo, African lutes had a rounded neck while the banjo has a flat neck - many slaves were carpenters, perhaps this innovation was influenced by the guitar that they witnessed Europeans playing. An African tradition that continued was the use of stretched animal skin over a drum in order to resonate, rather than the hollow wooden resonator. Though technically this was a complicated way to build, it would have been familiar to Africans and was retained with the banjo.

Attempts were made to reproduce the balafon in the Caribbean, it is an intricate build requiring specific types of wood and curing. It didn't thrive in the way the banjo did, which were easier to reproduce and make in the Caribbean.

The British author Richard Ligon (1585–1662) travelled to Barbados in order to make his fortune. He was dismissive of the slave music he encountered but wrote extensively on it. He brought with him a theorbo, a large Italian lute, and interacted with a slave musician called McCaw, who was recognised as the musical leader in his community and afforded privileges such as being allowed to come into the places of the colonists. Ligon witnessed McCaw building a lute, and his prejudices meant he documented an uneducated man attempting to replicate the theorbo. Ligon had no awareness that McCaw would have seen similar instruments in Africa. It is likely a prominent slave head musician would have had a deep understanding of musical traditions and be a multi-instrumentalist, if McCaw was born in Africa he would have had a depth of knowledge and musical education that would have equated to or surpassed that of a man like Ligon. This is a unique instance documenting the construction of a refined musical instrument by an enslaved Caribbean musician.

Sounds survive, if instruments could not be replicated they would find ways to replicate the sounds. One example of a sound that was recreated is the quills - a panpipe instrument traditionally made in Africa from large porcupine quills, this instrument was more widespread in the Deep South of the USA plantations. The material construction changed, but the terminology harkens back to the traditional African instrument.

Richard C. Rath (2005) writes how when drums and horns were banned, slaves were encouraged to play the fiddle - especially in the eighteenth century. They adapted the playing style so that drumming patterns were brought to the instrument. There was incredible ingenuity and innovation by the African diaspora transferring sound styles and patterns to instruments and also to the body – for example, patting juba, a tradition to use one's body as a drum. Scatting is one such method that has survived as a twentieth century example, used in jazz styles. These are deep historic traditions of sonic knowledge that transcend Africa and the diaspora. In the Caribbean the instrumentation adapted due to the harsh conditions so that new methods of sonic innovation emerged.

The reason for the emergence of the Caribbean musical styles is that they were intended to cross boundaries and connect people, it has created a global soundtrack, we can see this today in the spread of Black-Atlantic or Afro-Atlantic music. At its core, the purpose of the music was to cross boundaries and to connect people in a fragmented state from very different contexts. The music that originated in the Caribbean was able to move and influence the culture of the Europeans. Its original purpose was community building and this has continued as the music has travelled to other settings.

Irish And African Connections

Interactions between Irish and African people would have occurred on certain islands, but there is very little evidence to describing the communication that would have taken place. We can speculate that they would have brought their music and communicated. This is based on nineteenth and twentieth century knowledge where it is more apparent that crossover occurred. What is certain is that there was a circulation of Irish and African people in the slavery era and this would have included musicians.

With little on record to document the interactions between Irish and African people it is difficult to say how much the two cultures influenced and fused with each other. What is known is that by the late eighteenth century there were Irish and African-born people having relationships. Family life would have provided the ideal space where traditions could have mixed as in both traditions music and dance was deeply ingrained into social life.

The prejudices of the travel writers are revealing in stating how the Irish and Africans were perceived, as Meleisa Ono-George (interview 2019) noted Irish and African people were often racialised in the same way. Written by the English explorer Richard Jobson, *The Discovery of the River Gambra* (1623) is one of the earliest accounts of African music. Of musicians in the Gambia river region Jobson wrote: "it's a perfect resemblance of the Irish rhymer" commenting on the way musicians sat and played. This exemplifies there was a connection in the perception of listeners between the music of Irish and Africans.

It is well-documented that music was developed to accompany collective labour. In some situations, it allowed labourers to work at a steady, slow pace, and lift their spirits.

People were working alongside each other in the fields, both transported against their will. As stated previously, we know of rebellions where the Africans and Irish united. If those solidarities happened culture and music must have played a role.

The Banjo In Irish And Caribbean Music

The chapter on "Music, Culture and Survival" briefly looked at how the banjo may have developed as an instrument on the Caribbean plantations. This chapter will "fast forward" and look at how the banjo became an integral part of two very different musical styles from Ireland and the Caribbean.

A version of the banjo circa 1840 (credit: Metropolitan Museum of Art)

The Banjo In Traditional Irish Music

By the late eighteenth century and early nineteenth century the modern banjo was developed, writers of the time transcribed the instrument as the "bonjaw", "banjer" and "banjar". It remained a black instrument until Robert McAlpin Williamson, the Texan Supreme Court Justice, was documented as the first white banjoist when he played on stage in the 1830s.

It was the minstrel shows (that later became associated with racial stereotypes) that introduced the banjo to Britain, Ireland and France in the 1840s as the American group the Virginia Minstrels toured the country. One of the group, Joel Walker Sweeney had antecedents from Mayo in Ireland and claimed to have invented the fifth string on the banjo, though there are paintings that predate this claim that show banjos with five strings. It is likely these instruments contain the "chanterelle" known as the drone string, if Sweeney really did add a string it is likely this would have been another lower melodic string. Winans and Gibson (2018) pointed out that "outlandish claims have been made about Sweeney, from his being the 'inventor' of the banjo to his being the first white man to play the banjo. These claims are part of an effort, beginning in the nineteenth century, to divorce the banjo from its African American origins."

However Sweeney did extend the popularity of the banjo to audiences across the USA and Europe. It is likely that the five-string banjo was the instrument that was introduced to Ireland. Mick Maloney (1986) noted that a nineteenth century sketch exists of Captain Francis O'Neill's *Irish Minstrels and Musicians* that shows banjoist John Dunne where a fifth string and peg is clearly visible.

The minstrel banjo did not have frets and it was not until 1878 that these were added to commercially produced instruments, an innovation credited to Henry Dobson of New York State. It took a few decades before this development became common in all banjos, so it is likely the first Irish banjos were fretless. At this time the instrument was plucked or strummed with the fingers which indicates it may have been used to play simple melodies or rudimentary accompaniment.

When steel strings were developed and the plectrum used by mandolin players was used then then banjo players began to experiment more with the instrument. The short drone string was removed and manufacturers produced four-string banjos with twenty two frets. Around 1915 the tenor banjo was invented, this had seventeen or nineteen frets and a shorter neck. This style of instrument was first used to accompany Latin American dances but was later favoured by musicians playing Vaudeville, Music Hall, Dixieland Jazz and Swing. The five-string banjo which was not used commonly, with the exception of Appalachian musicians, was later restored to popularity with the Bluegrass revival.

The first Irish banjo player to record commercially was Mike Flanagan, born in Waterford in 1898, who emigrated to the USA at the age of ten. Similar to many Irish banjo players in the twentieth century, Flanagan started playing on the mandolin and taught himself the banjo as it was difficult to find a teacher to learn from. He recorded with his brothers Louis, who played harp, and Joe, who played the accordion. As the 1920s dawned more Irish musicians picked up the banjo and played reel, jig, and hornpipe melodies. Other banjo players of the period included Michael Gaffney (from New York) and Neil Nolan (from Maine) who played in Dan Sullivan's Shamrock Band in Boston. The music was played for lively dances and the musicians were required to perform both American and Irish music, hence why a tenor player often featured in the band. Typically these musicians used a CGDA tuning.

The 1960s saw a folk revival in England and Ireland, with The Dubliners enjoying international success fusing guitar-backed vocals with traditional Irish reels and jigs. Barney McKenna played tenor banjo in the group and inspired a new generation of banjoists so that the instrument is now an integral part of traditional Irish music. Most players also use the same GDAE tuning as McKenna that has now become the standard in Irish music. McKenna calibrated his banjo this way so that it was easier to play music in the keys favoured by flautists, fiddlers and pipers.

The appeal of the instrument can be attributed to the construction method favoured by African craftsmen, using animal skin to cover the body which acts as a resonator. Though today synthetic materials are more often used, this made the banjo loud enough to be played above the dance halls din or in noisy pub settings.

The Banjo In Mento Music

The classic rural style mento music had an acoustic, informal and folksy style according to Michael Garnice (2018). It is referred to as "country music" in Jamaica and the typical instruments included banjo and also the acoustic guitar, a home-made saxophone, clarinet or flute made from bamboo, a variety of hand percussion and a rumba box (also known as a marimbula).

The four-string banjo is the main instrument in mento. Usually a tenor banjo tuned in some kind of fifths tuning, although not always to concert pitch. If a tenor was not available, musicians used a five-string banjo and removed the 5th string - either capoed up or tuned in a "uke" tuning (essentially making it a plectrum banjo).

Due to its volume and sharp tone, the banjo's role in mento was both as rhythm and lead. When used as a rhythm instrument the banjo strummed in a similar fashion to how the guitar was used in reggae. In this respect the mento songs sound like an early version of reggae as they had a similar beat. Although the banjo was rarely used in reggae songs, the guitar sound used in reggae sounds like it may have been derived from the banjo playing style found in earlier mento music.

The banjo was used in a variety of ways as a lead instrument, sometimes played precisely and sometimes very loosely. As Garnice states: "it could riff wildly, or be played as orderly and pointillisticly as a music box. Sometimes it chimed like a steel drum, other times it sounded like a mandolin. But banjo always brightened up the song. One thing mento banjo doesn't sound like is the banjo playing heard in bluegrass or other American musical traditions".

The acoustic guitar in mento was typically strummed as a rhythm instrument. The banjo or winds usually performed any soloing. Banjo players were given "breaks" between the verses to improvise arpeggio-based solos that harmonised with the primary chords and suggested the rhythm. These lead melodies often varied between eighth notes and quarter-note triplets creating a polyrhythmic banjo phrasing over the choppy upstroke of the guitar strum.

As R&B music became more popular in the 1950s and 1960s, the banjo and the other instruments used in mento (bamboo instruments, clarinet, rumba box, flute, fife and penny whistle) were heard less often in Jamaican music.

The other style of mento that Garnice identifies was the urban mento style that looked to the 1920s Caribbean jazz bands for inspiration. The music was more urban, polished and had a jazzy dance band style. Often these artists used the word "orchestra" in their act name. Commercially manufactured saxophones, clarinets, basses and electric guitars were used in favour of banjos and home-made instruments.

One of the best and most influential mento banjo players was Moses Deans, who was an original member of mento's best known group The Jolly Boys, who formed in 1945. The band enjoyed commercial success in the 1980s and 1990s and Deans' banjo playing can heard on the Jolly Boys' albums *Pop 'N' Mento, Sunshine 'N' Water*, and *Beer Joint & Tailoring*. Another notable mento banjoist was Nelson Chambers who was co-founder of The Blue Glaze Mento Band. Chambers' banjo licks can be heard on Stanley Beckford's two essential mento albums - *Plays Mento* and *Reggaemento* that were recorded in 2002 and 2004. Chambers also performs on Blue Glaze's 2011 album *We Will Wait*, one of the last recordings he made before his death.

Louie Culture's 2004 track *Donkey Back* features a prominent banjo riff along with synthesized flute and lyrics filled with country proverbs. In that same year the "Chaka Chaka" dancehall "riddim" became popular that featured the banjo along with harmonica, fiddle swoops (though played on guitar), a bass line simple enough for a rumba box. The music had a pre-reggae beat and dancehall style. Artists such as Beenie Man, Elephant Man and TOK used the riddim several times.

Appalachian Music

A tradition that incorporates the banjo as well as influences from Africa and Ireland is Appalachian music. The musical style can be divided into two periods according to Debby McClatchy (2000): the traditional music that was brought over by Anglo-Celtic immigrants - ballads and dance tunes that were in evidence in the early eighteenth century; secondly, the "old time" music that was popular around 1900 to 1930, this music blended tradition with parlour and vaudeville music, African-American styles, and Minstrel Show tunes.

From the 1780s most of the early European settlements began in Pennsylvania, Irish and Scots came initially as indentured servants, when their period of servitude ended they went south to the mountains as the local land was too expensive for them. The Appalachian Mountains are characterised by their steep ridges and entangling foliage that makes the area difficult to transverse. The soil in the valleys is generally unsuited to agriculture. Life in this harsh environment was tough and communities isolated due to the terrain. Music was one way in which social cohesion was maintained and tradition passed down.

Traditional Appalachian music is mostly based upon Anglo-Celtic folk ballads and instrumental dance tunes. The former were almost always sung unaccompanied, and usually by women, narratives that told of female struggles such as *Barbary Allen, Lord Thomas and Fair Ellender*, and *Pretty Polly*. The content of the ballads changed to reflect the American context and locations, but many ballads still spoke of Lords and Ladies and castles. The more explicit lyrics were modified to conform to the morals of the more puritan churches that were found in the USA, as were any references to sin or paganism. Broadside ballads were written by professional composers and tended to speak of male working experiences and tragedies.

The call and response tradition in Appalachian music was influenced by traditions from the African slaves. Group singing took place at work and during worship, usually with one person leading and the rest responding. The lyrics were constantly updated and improvised to keep up the group's interest. The revival spiritual songs sung by white congregations were a direct descendant of this African tradition. After emancipation black music was discovered by mainstream USA and parlour songs known as "race music" became popular in the 1920s. Contemporary Appalachian songs allude to "children" toiling in the fields or "mother" having being changed from "pickaninnies" or "Mammy".

The instrumentation of the Appalachians started as Anglo-Celtic dance tunes but was reshaped by African rhythms and the introduction of new instruments. At first the fiddle was the main instrument. Originally it was played slowly to accompany the ballad lyrics. It is thought that the "reel" originated in the Scottish highlands in the mid-eighteenth century. Neil Gow, a Scottish fiddle player in the 1740s, is credited as the musician who developed the short bow sawstroke technique, playing in a powerful and rhythmical style that became the foundation of Appalachian mountain fiddling. Irish pipe playing also influenced the music, with the drone sound replicated by playing two strings on the fiddle. By the late-nineteenth into the early-twentieth century popular music, such as ragtime, influences could be heard and fiddlers also adopted classical music tunings to vary the sound of the instrument. Songs and dances changed to reflect the musical innovations as square dancing was adopted and tunes had words in places so the fiddler could have a break.

After the American Civil War ended in 1865, the banjo found its way to the music of the Southern Mountains. The guitar was added in 1910. With these additional instruments the songs became more melodic and elaborate. In earlier compositions the fiddler played in a more rhythmic style, but with other instruments providing a rhythm or chords the songs became more refined.

In the 1920s Henry Ford sponsored national competitions for "old-time" music and American audiences showed an interest in fiddling music. Eck Robertson in 1922 was the first rural performer to record his music. Many other acts followed and were able to make a career out of being musicians such was the popularity of the sound at that time. Tunes evolved to be shorter and more radio-friendly. There was a greater degree of crossover with popular music as the twentieth century saw the Appalachian region becoming less isolated.

Banjoist Charlie Poole's music was based upon parlour pieces, race songs, and vaudeville material, with the guitar and finger-picked banjo following each other in carefully orchestrated progressions. Gid Tanner and the Skillet Lickers played spontaneous music with multiple fiddlers and a raw sound heard in earlier string bands. Singing was usually a single male voice; the duet harmonies became more prevalent during the 1930s. Ma Maybelle of the Carter Family introduced a guitar style where lead melodies were picked out by the thumb.

The 1930s and 1940s saw artists such as Hank Williams and the advent of Brother Groups like the Delmores, the Stanleys, and the Louvins The introduction of swing, horns and electricity further developed the sound and laid the foundations for modern commercial country and western music.

Bluegrass developed in the 1940s from a mixture of several types of music that included old-time, but also country and blues. Bill Monroe and his band, the Blue Grass Boys, are credited with the creation of the style. One of the defining characteristics of bluegrass - the fast-paced three-finger banjo picking style - was developed by Monroe's banjo player, North Carolina native Earl Scruggs. Mary Caton Lingold (interview 2019) stated that so much of what makes bluegrass particular are blue notes and the blues scales which were created by African musicians. The pre-bluegrass Appalachian string styles under appreciate the influence of West African fiddlers whose styles combined with other traditions. The musicologist and expert on West African fiddle-playing, Jacqueline DjeDje has written about the influence of West African fiddlers coming from several streams of traditions. Thanks to musicians like Rhiannon Giddens and the Chocolate Drops the awareness of the African and black roots of Southern American folk music is increasing. But there is unwillingness by a lot of people to acknowledge the African influence on a white southern tradition. In parts of the Deep South of the USA. Irish-ness has been upheld over and above the African influence.

The Bog Trotters Band, photographed in Galax, Virginia in 1937 (credit: The Lomax Collection at the U.S. Library of Congress)

Traditional Appalachian music is still played today with Virginia, West Virginia, and North Carolina being notable places to experience the old-time folk music. Fiddlers' conventions, house parties and impromptu jams keep the music alive.

PART 2: PRESERVING AFRICAN CULTURE: FROM THE MAROONS TO REGGAE

"The warrior fights with courage not with anger."

Ashanti Proverb

"This world was not created piecemeal. Africa was born no later and no earlier than any other geographical area on this globe. Africans, no more and no less than other men, possess all human attributes, talents and deficiencies, virtues and faults."

Haile Selassie I (1963 address to African Leaders)

"Emancipate yourselves from mental slavery; none but ourselves can free our mind."

Bob Marley (*Redemption Song*, 1980)

The Maroons: A Brief History

Musical styles clearly descended from musical traditions bought to the Caribbean by enslaved Africans have been perpetuated and widely used by people of African descent as a means of finding a collective identity. In order to understand the music that was to take root in the Caribbean in the twentieth century we will look at the unique history of the Maroons in Jamaica. Their struggle of resistance and rebellion set a precedent that led to greater freedoms for the black population. In addition their retention of particular African cultural traditions had a profound influence on the music forms that followed into the twentieth century.

When the Spanish lost control of Jamaica to the British conquest that commenced in 1655, many slaves on the island seized their opportunity in this transitional period to flee to the hills and fight to the death for their freedom. Initially the Maroons sided with the Spanish but as it became apparent they would lose control of Jamaica a group led by Juan de Bolas assisted the British in the decisive raid that finally expelled the Spanish in 1660.

Slaves of the Spanish formed the first Maroon communities, also made up of free black people, former slaves and what remained of the Arawaks - a peaceful, domestic, agricultural people living on the island when the Spanish arrived. The name Maroon, of both Spanish and French derivation, means "hunters of wild animals" and later simply "wildness and fierceness".

The Maroons successfully resisted British attempts at re-enslavement for decades. In 1663 Governor Lyttleton signed the first treaty with the Maroons, granting de Bolas and his people land on the same terms as the British settlers. The authorities paid de Bolas and his men to hunt other Maroon communities and recent runaway slaves. The initial Maroon groups changed over the years as their numbers dwindled, migrated or merged with the settlers.

The Maroon communities became havens for runaway slaves, mostly Ashanti prisoners-of-war, an ethnic group native to the Ashanti region of modern-day Ghana. In 1690 a rebellion involving

500 slaves established the best organised Maroon group. The society was organised according to the highly militarised Ashanti polity. Outsiders were only admitted after a strict probationary period. The most famous leader of the western Leeward Maroons was Cudjoe. The Windward Maroons had settlements on the east of Jamaica and by 1720 they were led by Queen Nanny, who was born to Ashanti people but who escaped after being transported to the Caribbean. The Maroons were fearsome fighters who practised guerrilla warfare, using camouflage to surprise their enemy.

Cudjoe Making Peace with Colonel John Guthrie (illustration from 1803)

Known as the First Maroon War, the British launched a campaign against the Maroons from 1731 – 1739. Stalemate ensued and the authorities signed a peace treaty with Cudjoe in 1739 and with Quao of the Windward Maroons in 1740. Land and political autonomy was granted, in exchange the Maroons pledged allegiance to The Crown and to return runaway slaves in return for a bounty.

The Maroons were called upon to honour their treaties in 1760 during the slave uprising led by Tacky, they did intervene but were not fully committed in the skirmishes. Escaped slaves were captured, but often the runaways established their own communities.

To those who criticize the Maroons for their role in suppressing slave revolts and returning escapees to their slave masters Bilby (2001) makes the point that "those who dwell on this aspect of the past almost invariably fail to point out that the British policy of divide and rule cut both ways, and that the greatest threat to Maroon survival before the treaties of 1739 was posed by slave troops who, in exchange for promises of freedom and other enticements, fought alongside the whites in their attempts to annihilate the Maroon populations in the interior."

The Second Maroon War (1795-1796) saw the defeat of the community based at Cudjoe's Town (Trelawny Town). Following their surrender to the forces of Governor Balcarres the Maroons were deported to Nova Scotia and then to Sierra Leone. When they arrived in Africa they joined the "African American founders" and helped establish the settlement in Freetown.

In the present day the Maroon communities are autonomous to an extent, the isolation used to their advantage by their ancestors means their towns are among the most inaccessible in Jamaica. Accompong Town, Moore Town, Charles Town and Scott's Town are the locations of the official Maroon towns, dating back to the land promised in the 1739 treaties. The Maroons have retained their traditions, many of which are West African in origin. Tourists and native Jamaicans are invited to attend some events, while others are secret and remain a mystery.

In our interview with Ellen Campbell-Grizzle she stated that her father grew up in a Maroon community. The oral history tradition continues and has been taught to her, it is in this way that the culture of West Africa and the Ashanti has survived in the Caribbean. The Maroons also teach the significance of the treaties and defending the lands they won. Tensions over the treaties arose in 1962 when Jamaica gained independence and the new government did not address the political status of the Maroons. The assumption was they would be rendered null and void but the Maroon communities have resisted attempts to divide the territories or to reduce autonomy.

The Maroon towns are unusual in Jamaica, a country with one of the highest murder rates in the world, as there is virtually no crime and there are no police. The close knit community assures of safety by only admitting outsiders if they have the permission of the leader of the town.

The history of the Maroons is significant in terms of the influence it had on music. As Carter R. Stowell (2000) concludes the specific musical practices of Maroon communities are largely unknown or undocumented, the modern Maroon people maintain clearly neo-African practices. It can be assumed that these were passed from the early Maroons through oral histories as is common of both African and European folk traditions. The Maroons lived with greater freedom than their enslaved brethren and were best equipped to steward cultural practices through the turbulent environment of colonial Jamaica. Roger Bastide (1972) states the *bossales* - African-born slaves - were the ones "responsible for the preservation of African customs". Further, Maroon efforts set a precedent for attitudes of resistance which slowly progressed toward greater freedoms for the black population. Freedom appears to play a critical role in the natural preservation of cultural practices, at least in Jamaica.

The Culture of the Maroons

The Maroons greatly contributed to the foundation of the reggae and dancehall music genres, while still maintaining their unique musical traditions. This topic has been researched by the Granny Nanny Cultural Group who cite the work of Kenneth Bilby, one of the most respected anthropologists and ethnomusicologists who studied the Jamaican Maroons, particularly those of Moore Town.

The Maroons created forms of artistic expression, drawing upon their African, European and native Caribbean heritage, but emerged with something new and unique. "Kromanti" is at the heart of Maroon music and rituals, during these ceremonies participants experience "Myal", whereby they are possessed by spirits of their ancestors. Music and dances in this altered conscious state is comparable to other African traditions.

In his work *Music of the Maroons of Jamaica* and *Drums of Defiance* (1981), Bilby divides Jamaican Maroon dance and music into two main types: A "pleasure" style called "Yanga" and a "business" style called "Nyaba." The "lighter" or "less powerful" categories of Kromanti music "used primarily for recreational group dancing" include songs in genres such as "Jawbone", "John Thomas", "Sa Leone", and "Tambu", which are dominated by words from English, Jamaican creole (Patois), or the more rural and ritual version of Patois spoken by Maroons.

Bilby states the often "mournful themes and very moving, plaintive melodies" of Jawbone commentate on historical and everyday experiences of Maroon life. They are also used as work songs or "digging tunes" during the communal cultivation of farming lands. Sa Leone (named after the country of Sierra Leone) songs are normally topical in nature and are usually referred to as "woman songs", the dance styles are typically performed in ring formation.

The "heavier" and "deeper" category of songs incorporate more African-derived words and phrases. These songs are used mainly to invoke "Myal" whereby the dancers are possessed by the spirits of their ancestors. The ritual was accompanied by a specialist, guardian of community and ancestral knowledge known as the "Fete-man". Songs in this category include "Dokose", "Ibo", "Kromanti", "Mandinga", "Mongola" and "Prapa" – the names associated with various African societies. Each category of Maroon music has a distinctive style of drumming. Kromanti (also known as "Country") songs refer to a slave port in what is now Ghana. The music style is deeply spiritual, connecting to the world of the ancestors. The lyrics are dominated with words from the Ghanaian dialect, Akan Twi.

The Kromanti Dance uses drums fashioned from goat's skin that is beaten with the hands. Two drums are played, a lead and a supporting "rolling" drum. The drummer is known as the "Printing-man," "Okrema," or "Okrema-man," and occupies a place of secondary significance only to the Fete-man during the Kromanti Play. Other percussive instruments - the Kwat (bamboo played with sticks) the Adawo (a machete or pitchfork struck by iron) – compliment the drums. In the more spiritually potent Ibo, Dokose, Mandinga and Prapa category of songs the Abaso tick (a special style of stick), shakers and Paki (calabash gourde containing sticks) are also used. The Abeng is a side-blown cow's horn that was traditionally used as an instrument of war. For the Maroons it is used as a means of communication as well as in music.

Accompong Town Maroons also have a tradition of processional music that is a fusion of traditional African and older European military-style drumming. The style resembles the multiple drums and percussive instruments used in other Afro-Jamaican syncretic traditions such as Revival and Jonkunnu.

Many of the Maroon songs are homages to their leaders. Queen Nanny is a venerated figure in Jamaica, officially recognised as a National Hero of Jamaica, many compositions celebrate her memory and legacy. In most, but not all, Maroon songs women tend to sing the choruses. Schnapps and white rum is also used in Akan ceremonial and ritual practices, used by the Jamaican Maroons as an aid to ancestral communication during Kromanti Dance.

Though some Maroon musical and dance styles are identified with certain West African societies such as the Mandinga and Ibo, Bilby adds a note of caution to state "this should not be taken to mean that the songs which go by this name can be traced to this specific region of Africa. The derivations of Maroon musical styles and songs are difficult to pinpoint, and in most cases they must be seen as New World creations, the end results of a unique process of musical syncretism which long ago began to blend elements from a diversity of African traditions into new styles."

The role of the Maroons in maintaining African cultural traditions cannot be understated and it was this heritage the mento and reggae artists of the twentieth century drew upon - the complex African folk rhythms are a distinct feature of these styles.

Jamaican History: From Slavery And Rebellion To Rastafari

The population of Jamaica is made up in the main of people from the Gold Coast and Nigeria regions in West Africa and Congolese-Angolan people from Central Africa. East Indians, Chinese and European people make up the minority groups. The island was treated as a plantation society, cultivating sugar in the seventeenth century meant the population was primarily made up of African slaves. There was a constant influx of labour transported from Africa with these people bringing their music and knowledge with them. In 1807 the British ceased the importation of slaves. When the slave trade ended contact with Africa ceased, enabling Jamaican musicians to apply their own creativity to the music. However the institution of slavery still persisted until emancipation in 1834.

The British feared the collapse of the Jamaican economy so a system of apprenticeship followed, only the slaves younger than six years and older than seventy were given their freedom immediately. Most black Jamaicans remained on the plantations awaiting the release of their family members. The former slaves purchased land from the British, but the plots were too small to grow a great number of crops on. Those who left the plantations struggled to adapt and fell into impoverishment.

Black Jamaicans were unable to become immediately prosperous and Jamaican sugar production lagged behind the other Caribbean islands after slavery ended. This hardship cemented British views on black inferiority, James Walvin (1994) stated that this provided evidence to the former colonisers that "white races (and especially British) were superior to the black and the brown; that human differences were racially determined", with Jake Grace adding "this belief in superiority became even stronger than it was during slave times; those who believed in it felt that they now had scientific evidence to back it up".

In some areas Jamaica remained prosperous, the British continued to mine bauxite and sugar exports still remained the major export despite the decline. Some small businesses were able to export coffee to the USA, but many Jamaicans worked on the plantations that were re-labelled "estates". Wages were low and the work unreliable.

As the economy depressed in the following decades many Jamaicans were forced to return to the estates to work for the mainly British landlords. Workers were forbidden to export their crops by the land owners, a tactic that kept them impoverished. Tensions and conflicts arose over land issues leading to the Morant Bay Rebellion in 1865. Led by a Baptist preacher Paul Bogle, the rebellion was sparked when a black Jamaican was tried over trespassing on an abandoned plantation. Rioting broke out during the trial and a few days later Bogle and other protestors marched to Morant Bay court house. They were met by a militia who were forced to flee after the crowds turned on them, but seven protestors were killed as they retreated. Governor John Eyre sent government troops to crush the rebels, they killed indiscriminately 439 black Jamaicans died, many of whom were not involved in the protests. Bogle and 354 others were arrested and executed without a proper trial while many others were flogged or imprisoned and thousands of homes belonging to black Jamaicans were burned down. Businessman and politician George William Gordon, the son of a former slave woman and a Scottish planter, was critical of Governor Eyre's conduct during the rebellion. Despite not being involved in the protests Eyre accused Gordon of instigating the rebellion and after a hasty trial Gordon was executed for treason.

The years 1865 to 1930 saw the further decline of the sugar industry as it was never as profitable as it had been during the slavery era. It was impossible to meet the labour demand on the plantations unless the labourers worked for little or no wages. As this was occurring some entrepreneurial Jamaicans procured bananas from local producers and delivered the fruit to the ports, the exports became very popular in the USA. However, the United Fruit Company based in Boston soon monopolised this industry, which meant independent banana producers were bought out and workers had to return to the plantations to earn a wage.

Unemployment in Jamaica continued into the twentieth century with various movements looking to seek political and social change. In 1914 Marcus Garvey formed the Universal Negro Improvement Association and African Communities League. He also established the People's Political Party in 1929 and promoted the Back-to-Africa movement to encourage Americans of African origin to return to their ancestral homelands. In 1960 Garvey was proclaimed Jamaica's first national hero.

In the 1930s a new religion, the Rastafari movement, emerged among impoverished and socially disenfranchised black communities. Influenced by black nationalists such as Garvey, it presented an Afrocentric reaction against the dominant British colonial culture. The movement developed as Leonard Howell and several other Christian clergymen proclaimed that the crowning of Haile Selassie as Emperor of Ethiopia in 1930 fulfilled a Biblical prophecy. In the 1950s and 1960s the movement grew and became more noticeable. Rastas had uneasy relations with Jamaica's government, police and bureaucracy and were often arrested for cannabis possession, ritually smoked by practitioners. In the 1970s Rasta-inspired reggae artists such as Bob Marley increased the visibility of Rastafarianism. Middle class intellectuals such as the black nationalist Walter Rodney were also influenced by Rastafari philosophy. Rastafari became mainstream when Prime Minister Michael Manley used Rasta symbols and embraced the movement, he was endorsed by Bob Marley and other reggae artists.

Even when slavery was abolished a feeling of oppression persisted among black Jamaicans. The folk musicians and mento artists of the 1940s articulated the everyday struggle against poverty in their lyrics. These influenced the reggae musicians who followed later and embraced Rastafarianism giving a voice to the disenfranchised. Jamaica's National Heroes Paul Bogle and Marcus Garvey are celebrated in songs by reggae and dancehall artists such as Bob Marley, Burning Spear, Brigadier Jerry, The Cimarons, Steel Pulse and Prince Far I.

Reggae: A Fusion of African and European Musical Traditions

In his article *Harmony and Howling* Tim Marcus documented that the Europeans saw the Africans slaves as worthy of contempt, their music primitive and lyrical articulation as nothing more than a howl. Slave traders noted music was heavily ingrained in African culture, but perceived the sounds as unsophisticated as they were so unfamiliar to the European ear.

African music was non-notated, that is rather than being written down it was passed on through oral tradition. Excluding some folk music, most European music was recorded in musical notation so it could be played the same way each time. With music that is not notated there is more scope for the performer to improvise and vary depending on the context of each performance.

African music also contained a vocal pattern called call and response, usually alternating between a soloist and a chorus, the call and response was interactive. The chorus in response to the verse may not sound harmonious as it is based on un-tempered scales. European instruments usually had a specific note, for example each piano key sounds a particular note, un-tempered instruments like the human voice or fiddle can slide over pitches in between the pitches found on a piano keyboard. The diatonic and chromatic scales of European music do not include these notes. African music makes use of many more pitches so while the African ear heard harmonies in call and response, to Europeans at the time of the slave trade these structures and patterns were not heard. Some African music consisted entirely of drumming, sometimes to accompany call and response, this would also have been an unfamiliar sound to Europeans.

As the music was based on oral tradition, African music was normally based on based on reiteration of brief rhythmic and melodic patterns. It also often used irregular, as well as regular meters, sometimes their dances deviating from a count of four to a count of five. At this time European dance music rigidly kept to a constant meter.

With this in mind it is understandable that African music would have been radically different to the music white slave merchants were familiar with. This was the style of music that was transported to the Caribbean plantations.

Plantation masters often thought dances such as the Banboula, a Jamaican dance that was named after a drum used in the Calenda dance, to be quite distasteful as Father Labat noted in 1724: "From time to time they lock arms and make several revolutions always slapping their thighs together and kissing each other. It can readily be seen by this abridged description to what degree this dance is contrary to all modesty". Along with the music, African dance was quite different from what the Europeans were used to, however, in both cultures music and dancing went hand in hand.

The Europeans tended to encourage music and dancing during festive periods, usually giving the slaves a break at Christmas. Cynric R. Williams in his work *A Tour Through the Island of Jamaica from the Western to the Eastern End in the Year* (1826) wrote this passage to describe a musical celebration on Christmas Day stating the slaves "assembled on the lawn before the house with their gombays, bonjaws, and an ebo drum, made of a hollow tree, with a piece of sheepskin stretched over it. Some of the women carried small calabashes with pebbles in them and stuck on short sticks, which they rattled in time to the songs, or rather howls of the musicians." This exemplifies though the plantation masters encouraged African forms of music and dance, they did not understand it and the use of the word "howls" describes it in an animalistic context.

For the plantation owners African music and dance remained a curiosity and was generally disliked. Efforts were made to introduce slave musicians to European styles, training them to play fiddle and other more familiar instruments in slave ensembles for white society's entertainment. These musicians had higher status and were admired by their counterparts toiling in the fields, so that the European music they practised was imitated by the slaves fusing with African traditions.

By assimilating the European customs of their plantation masters the slaves could be gradually cut off from their African traditions. The resulting trauma of this degrading and submissive experience was that they became alienated from the homeland losing their heritage. African traditions were passed on by oral tradition, as these ties became severed so much was forgotten that the slaves lost a sense of their motherland and a sense of their history.

Elements of Jamaican music can be found in African and European music. The island is the birthplace of reggae, a genre that has its roots in the plantation experience. The two combating traditions exist in harmony within one music form. reggae draws upon history to provide an optimistic answer to the problem of oppression.

Styles found within African music are notable in reggae: call and response, repeating phrases and often feature vocal interactions with a larger group singing in harmony. The music is frequently based on a steady repetitive melodic and rhythmic patter throughout the song. The percussion is a feature that is uniquely African, there are usually multiple percussionists in reggae performances playing different and overlapping rhythms. Un-tempered scale tones are also employed, often created by the voice but also by brass instruments and horns.

These African traditions have been fused with European influences. Most songs are in the diatonic music scales that the Europeans used. Tempered instruments are used: guitar, piano and organ. Some reggae songs are based on European melodies. Most tunes are also composed in the common European 4/4 meter, where the style differs is that reggae places a particular emphasis on the count of three giving the music a distinct drive. In African-American music the stress can be heard on the two and four when this time signature is used.

Lyrically reggae artists have a desire to reconnect with their African roots and the lost history. To conclude with the words of Tim Marcus: "This music came out of a struggle between black and white, and the return to Africa reinforces the black nature of the music, almost subjecting the European tradition to a submissive role. In this respect reggae music is a response to the European traditions that were inflicted onto black slaves in Colonial times in an unjust manner."

Caribbean Musical Genres

Revivalism: Revival Zion and Pocomania

Revivalism began in Jamaica between 1860 and 1861 as a part of a religious movement called the Great Revival. It is a combination of elements from African pagan beliefs and Christianity and has several forms, the two major forms being Revival Zion and Pocomania. The Revival ritual involves singing, drumming, dancing, hand-clapping, foot-stomping and groaning along with the use of prayers to invite possession. It also includes music and songs from orthodox religion. Revivalism is found chiefly in the parishes of Kingston, St. Andrew, St. Catherine, St. Elizabeth and St. Ann.

Popular revival songs in Jamaica include *O let the power fall on me my Lord* and *River Maid*.

Mento

Mento is the original popular music form in Jamaica, developing during the plantation period and holding sway up to the 1950s. Mento had no special association with any particular community, region, religion, or social group. Blending very traditional music it could almost be described as Jamaican folk music.

The origins of mento are obscure, it was born out of the fusion of African and European influences. Its performance mode, rhythmic impulse, as well as its call and response type of singing is African in origin, while the scale patterns, harmonic concepts, and verse and chorus song types are European. The fiddle, flutes and guitars were core features of the musical style. To this could be added banjos, rhumba boxes (box instruments with plucked metal keys), drums, scriptures and other instruments wholly or partly of African origin.

The lyrics of mento songs often deal with aspects of everyday life in a light-hearted and humorous way, commenting on poverty, poor housing, and other social issues. Mento can be seen as a precursor to the dancehall music followed in the 1970s. At the peak of its popularity mento performances became a common feature at dances, parties and other events in Jamaica.

Mento is performed by an ensemble consisting of little more than a harmonica a few percussion instruments, by string bands featuring banjo and guitar, or even by large orchestras that include piano, drums, and a brass section. The musical style has also been associated with a genre of topical songs reminiscent of other Caribbean styles, such as calypso. Indeed, by the 1940s, mento was being influenced by a Trinidadian calypso (and was itself exerting an influence on the music of other islands).

Mento is regarded in some circles as the Jamaican equivalent to calypso. While some songs were aired regularly, others were banned as the lyrics were thought to be too sexually explicit or full of innuendo. Mento was first recorded by artists such as Louise Bennett, Count Lasher, Lord Flea, Laurel Aitken and Harry Belafonte, a New Yorker of Jamaican origin.

Calypso

Calypso is a style of Afro-Caribbean music that originated in Trinidad and Tobago during the early to mid-nineteenth century and eventually spread to the rest of the Caribbean, the Antilles and Venezuela by the mid-twentieth century. With a forward moving rhythm, its early forms bear a close relationship to mento. However the African heritage of calypso can be clearly identified. West Africans often sang songs of praise and songs of ridicule and mockery. Their professional street singers and community choirs performed these songs which relied on choral rhyme, the dancing chorus and the "call-and-response" order that are similar to native songs of the old Guinea coast. Even the name "calypso" or ("kaiso") can be traced to a West African source.

In 1912 Lovey's String Band recorded the first song that was identified as being of the calypso genre while they were visiting New York City. In 1914, the second calypso song was recorded, this time in Trinidad by Julian Whiterose, who was better known as the Iron Duke.

Rastafarian Music

Rastafarian music originated from the movement of the same name, which began during the 1930s in Jamaica. Count Ossie Williams set up a Rasta community in Kingston that welcomed many musicians and was very instrumental in the development of this music. His interest in music led him to take ideas from an easier type of Jamaican music called Burru which was originally from Africa. Count Ossie adapted the Burru drums and combined them with the Kumina rhythms of his youth in St. Thomas and arrived at what is now known as Rasta music.

Several instruments are played in Rasta music: tambourines, shakers, scrapers, striker bells, sometimes the saxophone and trombone and, most importantly, drums. Three kinds of drums are used: the largest is the bass drum which produces the steady rhythm then the fundeh which sets the pace of the music and finally the repeater which is the smallest of the three drums.

Ska

Ska, regarded as the forerunner of reggae music, was popularized by the late Don Drummond and the Skatalites during the early 1960s. It has been described as a Jamaicanised version of the North American rhythm and blues (R&B). The lyrics of ska were often about the prevailing socio-economic commentaries of the less privileged in the society. Popular songs of the ska era included Count Ossie's *Oh Carolina* and Millie Small's *My Boy Lollipop*.

The Ska dance

This consisted primarily of very fast paced movements such as "shuttle and split" which consisted of moving the hands upwards, downwards, side to side, backwards and forward while lifting the legs bent at the knees alternately.

Rocksteady

Rocksteady was a slower, somewhat erotic version of ska, with elements of American rhythm and blues and mento. Producers such as Duke Reid and Coxsone Dodd directed recordings with a slower beat and musicians such as Heptones and Alton Ellis were free to experiment with more complicated melodies. With the wider use of electronic instruments, horns were replaced by guitars – rhythm and solo – and the bass line became more complex and more melodic.

Rudie period

The transition period between ska and rocksteady was known as the "rudie" period. The songs of this period dealt with the criminal elements of the ghetto. Songs of the period included *007*, *Rude Boy* and *Rudie in Court* among others. Delroy Wilson, Bob Marley and the Wailers and Hopeton Lewis were a few of the many artistes of this period.

The dance

The ska and rocksteady dances were similar in movements. The main difference was the beat of the music. In rocksteady the dancer would try to keep the feet as steady as possible and then shift weight from one foot to the other slowly. At the same time the dancer would shake the shoulder to the beat of the music while rocking the rest of the body.

Reggae

Rocksteady had a fairly short life span. By the end of the 1960s the music had become more up-tempo and the popular musical genre known as reggae was born. Reggae is a slower version of rocksteady music and is characterised by its heavy, often repeated bass. Like its forerunners ska and rock steady, reggae songs often contain a message – political, religious or social. There is also a strong element of Rastafarianism in the music.

Reggae is based on ska and employs a heavy four-beat rhythm driven by drums, bass guitar, electric guitar and the "scraper" - a corrugated stick that is rubbed by a plain stick. The *Dictionary of Jamaican English* (1980) further states that the chunking sound of the rhythm guitar that comes at the end of measures acts as an "accompaniment to emotional songs often expressing rejection of established 'white-man' culture." Another term for this distinctive guitar-playing effect, skengay, is identified with the sound of gunshots ricocheting in the streets of Kingston's ghettos - skeng is a slang term for a weapon such as a gun or knife. Thus reggae expressed the sounds and pressures of ghetto life. It was the music of the emergent "rude boy" (would-be gangster) culture.

Reggae evolved from these roots and was characterised by politicised lyrics that gave a voice of the oppressed. The new reggae sound was characterised with its faster beat driven by the bass. Notable artists included Toots and the Maytals, who had their first major hit with *54-46 (That's My Number)* in 1968, and The Wailers (Bunny Wailer, Peter Tosh, and reggae's biggest star, Bob Marley) who recorded hits at Dodd's Studio One and later worked with producer Lee "Scratch" Perry. Jimmy Cliff gained international fame as the star of the movie *The Harder They Come* in 1972. This Jamaican-made film documented how the music became a voice for the poor and the dispossessed and helped spread reggae's growing worldwide popularity. Its soundtrack was a celebration of the defiant human spirit that refuses to be suppressed.

A connection grew between the music and the Rastafarian movement and reggae during this period of its development. Rastafarianism encourages the relocation of the African diaspora to Africa, deifies the Ethiopian emperor Haile Selassie I (his pre-coronation name was Ras Tafari) and endorses the sacramental use of ganja or marijuana. Rastafarianism advocates equal rights and justice and draws on the mystical consciousness of Kumina. As well as Bob Marley and the Wailers, other artists who popularised the fusion of Rastafarianism and reggae were Big Youth, Black Uhuru, Burning Spear and Culture.

In the 1970s reggae, like the ska music before it, spread to the United Kingdom, where Jamaican immigrants and also native-born Britons forged a reggae movement that produced artists such as Aswad, Steel Pulse, UB40 and performance poet Linton Kwesi Johnson. Reggae was embraced in the United States largely through the work of Marley, both directly and indirectly - the latter as a result of Eric Clapton's popular cover version of Marley's *I Shot the Sheriff* in 1974. Marley's career illustrates the way reggae was repackaged to suit a rock market whose patrons had used marijuana and were curious about the music that sanctified it. Fusion with other genres was an inevitable consequence of the music's globalization and incorporation into the multinational entertainment industry.

The popularity of reggae music has increased both locally and internationally. In 1983 the group Black Uhuru won the first Grammy Award with *Anthem*. Lovers rock, a style of reggae that celebrated erotic love, became popular through the works of artists such as Dennis Brown, Gregory Issacs, and Britain's Maxi Priest. Bob Marley, who died in 1981, was awarded the Order of Merit for his contribution to the development of reggae music.

Conscious Reggae

In 1993, there emerged a new dimension to reggae music. This was known as conscious reggae. The lyrics of these songs addressed social and spiritual issues. Artistes such as Tony Rebel, Sizzla Kalonji, Buju Banton, Luciano, Capleton and the late Garnet Silk fall into this genre.

Gospel

Locally, the term gospel can cover any expression of religious music. The words, rather than the music, determine the classification of the song. Most often the only uniquely Jamaican feature is the lyrics. Early gospel music in Jamaica was inherited directly from the United States of America. However, over the years, Jamaican gospel music has evolved.

One of the more popular proponents of gospel is the Grace Thrillers. Father Ho Lung and Friends have also contributed to the development of gospel, both in music and performance. Other popular gospel groups include the Love Singers, David Keane and the Sunshine Singers. New artists have also emerged through the gospel festival competitions put on by the Jamaica Cultural Development Commission, which has as its mandate the unearthing, training and showcasing of talent.

Deejay/ Dancehall Music

What began sometime in the 1970 (and blossomed in the 1980s) as a mere exhortation to the crowd to dance at a "session" led to the birth of deejaying. Deejays were a new set of champions of the music who spoke to the masses. Patrons at dances began to compare the ability of each deejay to motivate or "rock the crowd" and eventually this caught on, with artistes trying to "ride the rhythm" (chanting in tune with the beat), while at the same time creating with witty lyrics.

Thus deejay music became inextricably intertwined with dancehall. Dancehall became not just the place where a dance was held but the music itself. Deejay or dancehall music is sometimes considered vulgar and disrespectful to women as the language is at times sexually explicit and graphic. However because of strict rules for airplay set out by the Jamaican Broadcasting Commission the production of this type of dancehall music has lessened.

Deejays of the early days include Big Youth and Scotty. These deejays influenced the emergence of hip-hop music in the United States and also extended the market for reggae into the African-American community. In the 1980s and 1990s artists such as Yellow Man, Michigan and Smiley, Shabba Ranks, Beenie Man and Bounty Killer refined the practice of "toasting" (rapping over instrumental tracks) and were heirs to reggae's politicization of music.

Caribbean Dances

Jamaican traditional dances fall roughly under three categories: those that are African derived, those derived from European styles and creole, a mixture of both types. The African derived dances tend to be religious in nature, being integral parts in rituals and ceremonies. These dances take the ritualists into the realm of the spiritual and heighten their readiness for spiritual possession e.g. Kumina, Myal and Pocomania. The Maroon communities have preserved these aspects of Jamaica's African heritage.

Other dances derived from African culture were once of religious significance but are more often used in a social context, these include Etu, Quadrille and Maypole. Dances of European origin accompany work songs and ring games and are still performed today.

The creole dances that were created in Jamaica tend to borrow elements from both European and African cultures. The oldest and most popular of this type is Jonkunnu or Johnkannu, other forms are Bruckins, Pukkumina and Revival.

Bruckins

Bruckins is one of the creolised forms of traditional dances that reveals a unique mixture of African and European influences. The Bruckins party is a stately, dipping-gliding dance typified by the "thrust and recovery" action of the hip and leg. The dance was originally performed to commemorate the abolition of servitude on 1 August 1838. The form and content of the dance, with red and blue sets competing, is reminiscent of nineteenth century plantation Jonkunnu and the Set Girls' parade. The movement was said to have been derived from the Pavanne, which originated in Italy, a European court dance of the fifteenth and sixteenth centuries.

In Bruckins the pomp and ceremony of British royalty is mixed with African dance performance practices. The dance takes the form of pageant – a bright processional parade of people dressed as European royalty and other members of the royal court, courtiers, soldiers and other gentry. This was a direct imitation of what the newly-freed slaves saw as the Royal Family and their military complement.

The movement however is mainly African derived; the jotting forward of the pelvis, use of bent knees, flexed foot, tilted back torso and bent arms are all elements attributable to the dances of West Africa. A Bruckins party usually began late in the evening. Dancers, formed in two sets, proceeded from one house to another, parading their costumes and displaying their dance skills.

The two sets, one red the other blue, are rivals and often kept their costumes a secret until day of the celebration. The queens of each set came out first and had a dance competition for the duration of one song to see which would "bruck" the better. A tea time session followed, this section is not as common in the present day.

Bruckins includes music from the drum, knocking of the sticks, a fife and singing songs. The drummers and singers do not dance but move with the procession. Today Bruckins is found mainly in Portland, the eastern section of the island. The Jamaica Cultural Development Commission keeps the culture alive through holding festivals.

Burru

This particular form of dance is a fertility masquerade performed in Lionel Town and Hayes (Clarendon). It has familiar features to the Jonkunnu. The dance shows strong fertility elements as evidenced in the deliberate rotating action of the hip while bending through the knees accompanied by breaks of intermittent small jumps.

Dinki mini

Dinki mini is mainly found in St. Andrew, St. Mary and St. Ann. It is a member of the Wake Complex of traditional dances, performed after a death. Dinki mini is performed on the second to the eighth night of the traditional nine-long night observances. These sessions are primarily lively and celebratory in nature and are held to cheer up the bereaved. Dancing in couples and singing lively "mento" type of music takes place for the first few nights. During the performance the male dancer bends one leg at the knee and makes high leaps on the other foot. Both males and females dance together with very suggestive pelvic movements. An integral aspect of this dance is the use of the instrument called a benta.

Ettu

The Ettu dance is performed in the parish of Hanover and is a social dance from Africa. It is believed that Ettu is a corruption of the word Edo, the name of a West African Yoruba tribe (a west African society now located predominantly in Nigeria). The dance involves the lifting, and dropping of elbows and shoulders, with the feet doing sideways shuffling steps. The songs are short and repetitive, built on four notes only and sung in a Yoruban dialect.

Gerreh

The Gerreh is a dance of African origin that is performed the night after the death of a person. The dance is very lively and celebratory in nature and geared to cheering the bereaved. It is similar to the Dinki Mini and Zella with more emphasis being placed on the hip movements executed mainly by the female dancers. The instruments used in Gerreh are similar to those used in Dinki Mini with pot covers taking the place of the benta.

Gumbay

The Gumbay was also performed in the parish of St. Elizabeth and is derived from Myal. Gumbay was also the name of the healing cult from which the dance originated. The dance consists of a series of long steps followed by vibrating sideways body movements and by wheeling turns and sudden stops with pelvic forward tilt. During possession various feats such as back bending, rolling over in somersaults and climbing high coconut trees could be observed. This dance is well known among members of the Maroon population.

Jonkunnu

Jonkunnu is a band of masqueraders which usually perform in towns and villages around Christmas time. The costumes are of Akan origin, a region where Ghana is now located. The Jonkunnu customs go as far back as the days of slavery, but at that time the bands were larger and more elaborate. The band was made up of musicians who played tunes of well-known traditional songs on the fife accompanied by bass and rattling drums, shackas and graters.

The characters in the Jonkunnu band were usually played by men. Their faces fully covered and when they spoke it would be in coarse whispers as tradition told that no one should be able to identify them. Characters in the Jonkunnu masquerade were dressed in costumes to appear frightening to onlookers, with characters such as King and Queen, Cow Head, Horse Head, Devil, Pitchy Patchy, Red Indians and Belly Woman.

Kumina

From 1655-1816, the Church of England made no attempt to Christianize the slaves, according to Carter R. Stowell (2000), a policy that reflected the hypocrisy of the Church at that time with fears that Christianity would confer equal status upon the slaves. However nonconformist denominations — the Moravians in 1734, the Methodists in 1736, the Baptists in 1783 and the Presbyterians in 1823 - did find their way into the Jamaican slave communities.

A folk religion evolved out of a blend of African religions at the same time. The cult of Kumina was developed from the beliefs and traditions brought to the island by Bakongo enslaved people, from the Congo region of West Central Africa. Kumina ceremonies took place for births, deaths, marriages and other occasions involved vigorous dancing, drumming, a sacrifice, alcohol (typically rum) and ancestor-spirit possession. Drum rhythms summoned the spirits and the participants communicated with their ancestors.

The presence of the drum was a symbolic element, among the tangible connections to an African heritage. For the Ashanti the drum was the voice of God and a medium of worship. R.S. Rattray in his 1923 book *Ashanti* recounts their story about the origins of drumming: "The "Kokokyinaka" is a beautiful dark bird that frequents the forest... Its call is not unlike the notes of the drums. It is every drummer's totem, they claim clanship with it and would not eat or kill it. Its call is something like "Kro kro kro kro ko kyini kyini kyini kro kyini ka ka ka kyini kyini kyini ka". The Ashanti say it taught them to drum." Drumming is sacred to the Ashanti like the bird to the forest.

The Kumina drumming style had a great influence on later Rastafari music, especially the Nyabinghi drumming, and Jamaican popular music. Count Ossie (1926 – 1976) was a notable pioneer of the drumming style in popular music and it continues to have a significant influence on contemporary genres such as reggae and dancehall.

In time, the Caribbean people of African descent would combine elements of Christian and Roman Catholic beliefs with African folk religions. This led to a multiplicity of traditions throughout the Caribbean.

Maypole

Maypole, which is also referred to as the Long Ribbon Pole in rural areas, was a part of outdoor social festivals of old England and Jamaica and was performed at fairs, garden parties or picnics. It involves the plaiting of different coloured ribbons demonstrating three basic traditional patterns starting with the grand chain or "basket weave" wrapping the ribbons around the pole from the top. There are various styles in Maypole, more popular being the Spider Web, Flair, Dome and Umbrella.

Myal

Myal is one of the oldest dances in Jamaica and is associated with a type of religious observance that was mostly performed in the parish of St. Elizabeth. It was once associated with Obeah but recent research suggests it is derived from the Kongo religion, practised by the KiKongo people from the African Congo region. The dance involves a wide range of body movements, extensive use of space and exuberant actions. These are done by throwing the body on the ground and by acrobatic feats, as well as a vibrating movement brought about by a succession of rapid sideway shifts from foot to foot, on the toes and with knees bent.

Quadrille

Quadrille is a coupled (male and female) dance in Jamaica practised during slavery. There are three styles – the Ballroom Style, the Camp Style and the Contra Style. The Ballroom Style (or Square) of Quadrille originated from the popular dance of the French and English in the eighteenth and nineteenth centuries and highlighted the elegance and mannerisms of the elite of these societies. While the Camp style of Quadrille, also known as long way set formation, includes African elements and is known as the Afro-Jamaican version of the Ballroom Quadrille. The Contra Style Quadrille is performed only to mento music from beginning to end.

Tambu

The Tambu dance takes its name from the tambu drum and is performed mainly for entertainment with couples facing and moving towards each other using the Shay-shay, Saleone and Mabumba sequence. The Shay-shay features rotating action of the hips, shuffling along with one foot on the ball.

Zella

This folk dance form is rarely heard of but is similar in form and structure to the Dinki Mini as it forms part of the death observances and rituals in Portland. The difference is in the main instruments which is a pair of Kumina drums.

PART 3: MONTSERRAT: EMERALD ISLE OF THE CARIBBEAN

"Planted in these Montserrat sands
Are footprints many nations beat
My blood burns but I know not where
To plant my schizophrenic feet."

Sir Howard Fergus (*Footprints*, 1978)

"Oh people of Montserrat, you're all Cudjoe's kin.
You're the sons he begat – you are not born in sin.
Be strong; fight oppression; don't let Cudjoe die in vain
Uphold your Constitution; seek justice through pain.
Be not slaves to overspending, to corruption and greed
Be warriors for peace unending. Stand firm; with you I plead.
For Cudjoe was your father who died for you and me
That day, on St. Patrick's, when he hung from the tree."

Shirley Spycalla (*1768: The Slave Rebellion*, 2014)

Montserrat

Montserrat is known as the "Emerald Isle" of the Caribbean due to the Irish influence on its history and culture. Archaeological field work has indicated the island was populated by Arawak Indians, but by the time of Christopher Columbus' voyage of 1494 raids by Carib Indians had left the island devastated. Columbus gave the island its name after he noticed that it resembled the land around the Spanish abbey of Santa Maria de Montserrati. Montserrat was settled in 1632 by a British contingent from the mother colony of St. Kitts. The original colonists were English and Irish, the latter first came as indentured servants to work in the plantation system.

Later, Catholic refugees from Virginia, USA came to escape religious persecution. By 1648 there were one thousand Irish families on the island. In 1649 Cromwell sent political prisoners to Montserrat, increasing the population and helping to preserve its Irish character.

Sugar and slaves eventually changed both the economy and the culture. In the seventeenth century, after tobacco production waned, Montserrat developed into a typical plantation colony. By the 1650s African slaves began to arrive which was the time when the sugar industry on the island commenced. Slaves quickly outnumbered Irish indentured servants, and eventually labour on the plantations was predominantly African.

By 1705 a planter class, based on slave labour and sugar, was fully established. The planter class attempted to control and coerce the black population, leading to several rebellions, including the St. Patrick's Day rebellion of 17 March 1768.

Sugar fortunes began to disappear toward the end of the eighteenth century. Earthquakes, droughts, hurricanes, French raids and the loss of slave labour after emancipation in 1834 combined to end the plantocracy. Cotton supported the economy until the 1960s, when tourism and an elaborate real estate construction scheme were instituted.

Irish cultural retentions are largely symbolic. Some claim that modern-day Montserratians have an Irish brogue, but linguistic studies have shown this is not conclusive. The national emblem is a carved Irish shamrock adorning Government House, and the island's flag and crest show a woman with a cross and harp (see below). Other cultural survivals, such as a value systems, codes of etiquette, musical styles, and an Irish recipe for the national dish called "goat water" stew, are considerably more problematic as cultural legacies. Its history has left ruins of the plantation period as well as colourful houses in the capital city of Plymouth. However, the contemporary culture is pan-Caribbean with a heavy overlay of African and Anglo-Irish elements.

People today in Montserrat can trace their ancestry back to Ireland, often to unions between Irish and African couples that were more prevalent in the eighteenth century - though these were discouraged by the authorities. The island's patois is a mixture of words from Africa, Ireland, Europe and also from the language of the indigenous Arawak and Carib peoples.

From 17 March each year St. Patrick's Day is celebrated in a week-long festival with homage to African and Irish heritage. In 1768 slaves rebelled and the uprising was crushed by the authorities. By this time the Irish working classes were overseers and managers rather than labourers in the fields. The reason for the timing of the rebellion is that the plotters anticipated the British and Irish would be distracted by the St. Patrick's Day feast and festivities at Government House.

In the 1970s there was a renewed interest in this event and it became a celebration that made its way into the cultural landscape. It is one of the few places outside of Ireland where it is a national holiday. Sir Howard Fergus (interview 2019) noted that there are tensions on the island over to how to celebrate the event: in order to promote tourism there is an emphasis on Irish culture, dressing in green and pub crawls; but local scholars prefer to commemorate the nine rebel freedom fighters that were executed after the abortive uprising.

Emancipation Day is a national holiday that takes place on the first Monday of August - picnics, bazaars and dances are held to celebrate the day when slavery was abolished on 1 August 1838. Many parishes have village days, beauty contests, and calypso contests.

By 1995 the island had a population of about 10,000 but volcanic eruptions halved that number. The Soufrière Hills volcano, which had been dormant for centuries, erupted and half of the island was buried in more than twelve metres of pyroclastic flows and mudflows. The southern part of the island, including the capital city Plymouth, was destroyed leaving the area unsafe and uninhabitable.

The destruction and disruption to the economy caused over half of the population to leave the island. Volcanic activity has continued and an exclusion zone is enforced on the southern part of the island. The northern part of Montserrat has been largely unaffected and the new government centre is at Brades.

In 1998, the people of Montserrat were granted full residency rights in the United Kingdom, allowing them to migrate if they chose. British citizenship was granted in 2002.

PART 4: BARBADOS: TUK BANDS AND ART-MUSIC

"Fellow Men and Friends I have lived to see you declared free men and I hope ... to live and see you made free..."

Samuel Jackman Prescod

"The architecture of our future is not only unfinished; the scaffolding has hardly gone up."

George Lamming

"Every time I hear Mozart, Eine Kleine Nachtmusik and Beethoven Symphony No. 5 in C Minor - it brings to mind those beautiful childhood memories of back home around noon time. Memories of my Sweet Barbados."

Charmaine J. Forde

Tuk Bands And Landship

The history of Barbados is unusual in the respect that it did not undergo periods of rule by different European powers as occurred on the other Caribbean islands. Barbados was ruled by the British from colonisation in 1627 up until independence in 1966. Because of this Barbados was known as "Little England", the island's character reflecting as Bilby states "cultural homogeneity, 'puritanical' propriety and tidiness, and a relatively comfortable fit between imposed colonial culture and local identity."

There are two notable forms of uniquely Bajan musical performance, the first is the "tuk band", and the second is the "Landship". The tuk bands are a type of marching band, the ensemble consists of a double-headed bass drum, triangle, flute and a snare drum; the traditional fiddle has most recently been replaced by the pennywhistle. Landship performances are organised by friendly societies that stage "naval manoeuvres" along with marching, music and dance, the music is normally provided by tuk bands. Costumes are similar to those of the British Royal Navy.

Though on the surface these traditions appear to be derived from the British colonial influence, scholars such as Curwen Best (1999) and Marcia Burrowes (2005) have argued that these performances have been formed as a result of creolisation and that they represent a form of cultural "subversion" and "cloaking". African-Caribbean traditions were maintained in the face of a restrictive colonial environment where the opportunities of overt cultural expression and resistance were very much limited.

The tuk bands resemble the British colonial era military bands, but are accompanied by characters that are African in origin, using costumed figures to represent various elements. The Jonkunnu dance tradition found in Jamaica is similar in this respect with its various African-derived characters. In the tuk bands Shaggy Bear often makes appearances to celebrate bank holidays and represents an African witch doctor. The Donkey Man represents the old form of cart-pulled transportation, Mother Sally symbolises female fertility and the Stiltman is a figure who embodies surviving hard times.

Landship performances are theatrical dances that resemble the passage of ships through rough seas. The British naval influences can be seen in the costumes and structure of the dance, but the tuk band drummers play an African rhythm to accompany the dancers.

Art-Music

Caribbean music such as reggae and calypso has been documented by scholars and popular writers but Dr. Christine Gangelhoff has identified a much less examined style that is known as "Art-music". Numerous composers of art-music have emerged from the Caribbean who produce music in this tradition. Gangelhoff defines art-music as a form that has developed from the European classical traditions. It is distinct from the traditional and folk music styles as the music is arranged and written in the western staff notation rather than preserved by oral tradition. Though art-music may be inspired by folk music and popular traditions, the style is formal and the music structured. The composition and performance requires skills and knowledge unique to the classical style, interpretation rather than improvisation is the focus of the performer.

In the 1930s James A. Millington, a black New York-trained concert violist, performed at Barbados' St. Michael's Cathedral. He struggled to get through the crowds who were clamouring to be admitted and had difficulty explaining to them that he was performing as audiences expected classical musicians to be white. Millington was joined with British organist Gerald Hudson under the name "Black and White Whiskey Dogs" and the pair played concerts all over the Caribbean.

Millington also taught violin at his Spry Street studio. In 1949 he was appointed visiting master at Combermere School. In 1958 John George Fletcher, a highly skilled musician born of Grenadian and Scottish parents, was offered a similar position at Combermere and continued Millington's work, he spent thirty years developing the music program at the school. Fletcher travelled widely with his organ music and the choir of St. Michael's Cathedral. He made many friendships and invited talented organists from Europe and North America to play in Barbados in music exchange programmes.

Most of the music teachers in Barbados and the pupils studying use the Associated Board of the Royal Schools of Music (ABRSM). Established in 1889, this exam board for the Royal Schools of Music is a leading authority on musical assessment and a body which delivers over 650,000 graded exams and professional diplomas for more than thirty-five instruments, singing and music theory every year in ninety-three countries. The exams are accredited by the regulatory authorities throughout the United Kingdom and are part of the National Qualifications Framework. The ABRSM began examinations in the Caribbean starting with Jamaica in 1908 and in Barbados in 1926. John George Fletcher administered the exams from 1969 to 2000.

Appreciation of musical and cultural heritage is encouraged by the Barbados Ministry of Education, Youth Affairs and Culture through the Cultural and Historical Exposure for Kids in Schools (CHEKS) program. Those who have studied at Combermere include the jazz saxophonist Arturo Tappin, Joy Knight-Lynch - violinist and leader of the Barbados Youth Orchestra, organist Samuel Springer, James A. Millington and the internationally famous pop star Rihanna. Former alumni Sean Jackson serves as the Director of Music at Stanwich Church in Greenwich, Connecticut and performs organ concerts all over the world, he praised the school at Combermere school that "has produced many students over the years who excelled in music and [has become] known as the premiere secondary school in Barbados for music education".

Other notable Bajan musicians include the composer Roger Gittens who helped to write the study programme at the Barbados Community College Division of Fine Arts. Gittens has composed a wide variety of pieces ranging from calypso and jazz to gospel and choral music. The Barbados National Youth Symphony Orchestra, the Barbados Chamber Orchestra, The Myriad Singers of Barbados and the St. Leonard's Boys Choir provide opportunities for musicians to perform and for audiences to enjoy art-music. The Royal Barbados Police Force Band performs widely both nationally and internationally.

PART 5: CARRIBEAN AND IRISH MIGRATION TO SLOUGH

"Most countries send out oil or iron, steel or gold, or some other crop, but Ireland has had only one export and that is its people."

John F. Kennedy

"The Windrush-era experience marks that moment when the daughters and sons of former slaves, indentured labourers, colonised and other subjugated peoples undertook to expand the boundaries of peoplehood and democratic participation."

Harry Goulbourne

Caribbean migration to Britain

Following the Second World War Britain was short of workers, a generation of Caribbean workers answered the call for help and on 22 June 1948 The Empire Windrush arrived at Tilbury from the West Indies. Labour was needed across sectors, from raw material production to reconstruction, the service sectors, NHS and the public transport network.

People left the Caribbean for a variety of reasons, for some it was the lure of new job opportunities, others wished to escape societal oppression and poverty. Carmen Callaghan described her early years in Anguilla as idyllic with a strong emphasis on family life. However there were few job opportunities on the island so Carmen left for England in 1962.

Eustace Herbert came to England in 1962, he remembers a comfortable life growing up on St. Kitts, his father cultivated crops and owned a variety of livestock. His mother used to prepare food for the Con Phipps Estate, one of the former slavery-era plantations. Eustace stated relationships were important in this environment and the culture he grew up in was integral to shaping his beliefs throughout his life.

Many who arrived from the Caribbean had one mind set: they were going to go to England, work for about five years and return. When William Hylton left Jamaica in 1963 to come to Slough he had this plan in mind. He came to England after a friend of his told him of the work opportunities so thought he would try his luck. Eustace recalls that no matter which island people came from, even though people wouldn't have this conversation with each other, if you asked them how long they were going to stay they said for five years, almost like a subconscious mind. Carmen too stated this was her original intention, however as she became accustomed to her new environment she found she enjoyed the friendships she had made with other arrivals from various Caribbean islands and also those who came from Ireland, Wales, Scotland as well as English people. Eustace had the same intention but once he started laying down roots, finding work, making friends and creating links five years had gone by and any thoughts of returning to the Caribbean had disappeared.

Clinton Jack was motivated to come to England too, but in his case it was for greater musical opportunities. Coming from a musical family in St. Vincent, members of his family were part of one of the islands biggest family bands - The Jacks Brothers. Clinton intuitively picked up music at an early age teaching himself drums, trumpet, bass guitar, rhythm guitar, harmonica, violin, keyboards and piano. Frustrated by an inability to make enough earnings from his talents, Clinton left in 1962. He felt it was possible to achieve a level of fame on the island but often he was not paid what he was promised.

Caribbean migration in the nineteenth and early part of the twentieth century was dominated by men who left to work on agricultural and construction projects in the USA, Cuba, Panama and other parts of the Caribbean. The post-Windrush migration was notable for the high number of women who arrived, often accompanying or following their spouse. According to Nancy Foner (2008), by 1961 – 1966 the number of female immigrants exceeded that of male arrivals. This illustrated the ambitions and desire for independence held by Caribbean women.

This was exemplified when we interviewed Carmen, she told of her father often being away when she was growing up as he had to periodically leave Anguilla to find work. Carmen came to England as a teenager with nine of her friends. Her ship the SS Ascania completed its two week voyage and Carmen's brother greeted her when she arrived at Southampton.

Those that came over from the Caribbean arrived with a desire to work but they also brought their culture with them. When the Empire Windrush arrived from Jamaica one of the passengers was Lord Kitchener, a calypso singer from Trinidad. As he disembarked from the ship by chance a newsreel company was there to film and he treated them to a rendition of his song *London Is The Place For Me*.

Carmen Callaghan

Carmen is from a musical family, she was a member of the school and church choir in Anguilla, while her sister was the organist at the church. Her grandfather was an accomplished violinist and all of the children in her family learned to play an instrument. Her grandparents held soirées where her eldest sister would play the organ and everybody would sing along and dance. Family occasions involved singing along, birthdays and Christmases being notable for the big parties and musical celebrations.

St. Peter's Church often held cultural evenings where anyone was welcome to go up on stage to display their talents, be it singing, dancing or performing comedy. One night Carmen sang unaccompanied on stage. This proved to be a significant moment as in the audience were members of a band who were looking for a singer. They were so impressed that they approached Carmen at the end of the night and invited her to a rehearsal. The band comprised of Claude Richardson on drums, Evan Gumbs on guitar, Joe Fenton on rhythm guitar and Jim Charmers on bass. All the members had come to England from various Caribbean islands. The rehearsal went well and Carmen became the band's vocalist.

They called themselves The Interpreters and regularly played gigs. For Carmen this was a great way to explore Great Britain as they played the length of the country. In Slough they played at dances for the nurses and the police, also at hospitals and navy clubs. Carmen enjoyed every minute playing to enthusiastic audiences. After eight years The Interpreters folded as some members moved away from Slough and were finding it difficult to commit to keeping the band functioning.

Acting as Carmen's agent, Claude Brooks introduced her to the Tropic Isles Steel Band. Carmen knew most of the band, that included Eustace Herbert as a member, and this marked a new era in her musical career. The band was very active and played at all sorts of venues and occasions: London hotels, at Bar Mitzvahs for the Jewish community, again at the police dances and also travelled abroad to festivals in France and Portugal.

So many people had never seen or heard a steel band before and marvelled at the beautiful sounds that the pans made. Many could not understand where the sound came from and were looking for microphones and amplification.

When playing abroad audiences thought they were from the USA as they had never seen black people from England before. They regularly played to an audience in France of Creole people, who were from the West Indies or were the direct descendants of people from the islands. They thoroughly enjoyed the music and delighted in hearing Caribbean music mixed with contemporary pop.

American soul music was also popular at this time as was reggae so The Tropic Isles Steel Band learned to play different sounds to suit their audiences. They often played at elderly people's balls and were able to modify their sound to incorporate the slower dances, the waltzes and foxtrots, that these audiences preferred. At the end of each night, Carmen always felt like she had given a good performance. The band never got any negative feedback and people often asked for encores, making these years among the best of her life.

The steel pans that bands such as The Tropic Isles Steel Band played were created in Trinidad in the 1930s, but their origins go back much further. The previous chapters show that the enslaved Africans had a penchant for reinventing instrumentation, with the Caribbean authorities repeatedly proscribing the playing of drums believing they could be used to incite rebellion. This was the case in Trinidad after the 1877 Canboulay riots when drums were banned, the musicians replaced these playing bamboo sticks but these too were made illegal.

In 1937 musicians in Laventille began playing various dustbin lids, frying pans and oil drums. International popularity followed in 1941 when US soldiers stationed on the island took a keen interest in the music. After the war 55 gallon oil drums became the choice from which the steel pans were fashioned. The first time British ears heard the steel pans was in 1951 when the Trinidad All Steel Percussion Orchestra was formed to attend the Festival of Britain. This was the first steel band whose instruments were all made from oil drums, their line-up included the pioneers Ellie Mannette and Winston "Spree" Simon.

Eustace Herbert

Music was also a passion of Eustace's and he played in a steel band in his youth in the Caribbean. He continued this tradition when he came to Slough, joining the Tropic Isles Steel Band, which also featured Carmen Callaghan. He played in the band for over twenty five years and was grateful for the openings being a member of the act provided as they played big functions supporting the likes of the Joe Loss Orchestra, a popular musician in the British dance band era, and performed in front of heads of state and high ranking people.

When Eustace retired from playing music he didn't want the tradition to die out and in 1997 decided to start a new steel orchestra for the youth in Slough, open to any race, colour or creed. With the help of his former band mate, Robert Paris, Eustace purchased some steel pans that were for sale at Greenwich University. A meeting was held to consult with the young people who were interested in being involved and the Slough Youth Steel Orchestra was born.

Clinton Jack

Clinton Jack struggled to find his feet when he first came to England. He needed to find the right people and when he lived in London he found most musicians he played with didn't share his understanding and ability. He found it difficult to express himself and moved to live with his cousin in High Wycombe. It was there that he started a steel band. In the 1960s they played a lot of English pieces and Clinton enjoyed playing Irish pieces, *Danny Boy* being one of his favourite tunes.

Just as Eustace did in Slough, Clinton also continued the legacy of steel bands – in his case through teaching. He studied at Goldsmith University and graduated two years later. Required to do a work placement, Clinton opted to teach music in prison. For this work Clinton was commended by Princess Anne, who told him she enjoyed his music. He helped to get his lecturer Phil Mullan a role teaching offenders and was thanked for doing so as Phil found the work very rewarding.

Upon graduating, Clinton taught music at Henry Floyd Grammar School in Aylesbury. He taught the students to play steel drums and ensured they learned popular music pieces they were familiar with rather than calypso and reggae. During the Jubilee celebrations the band performed for the Queen with Clinton conducting. After ten years he left and was overwhelmed when the children and parents sent him leaving gifts.

Clinton's musical career in England also saw him join a group called Four Ways Drama. He was in the musical quartet and used to play double bass providing the backing music to accompany the plays. Musically he felt at home in this ensemble as the pianist was very accomplished and the two of them could play jazz together, improvising Nat King Cole and swing style music.

Clinton was able to earn much more money playing in England than he could have in the Caribbean. He worked for ten years playing bass in the resident band for a restaurant that was popular with celebrities. He met a host of famous people from that period that included Diana Dors, Mike Reid and Norman Wisdom. Clinton played three or four nights a week in a quartet enjoying his time with the band as they played jazz and other styles. There was a missed opportunity with Bob Monkhouse, who asked if the band would work for him on his popular ITV television show. Bob was very impressed that Clinton's band could follow the rhythm of his comedy routine knowing when to play music around his jokes. The band were all very keen but one member was unsure so the chance was missed.

Another musical culture that was introduced by the Caribbean arrivals was that of the sound system. The concept became popular in Kingston, Jamaica in the 1940s. DJs built their own systems consisting of a generator, turntables and speakers to play at street parties. The DJs played American music at the beginning, but began to favour local genres as time went on. Competition between DJs meant the music became louder and the speakers grew to the size of wardrobes. Part of the culture involved a clash whereby two DJs would battle each other in an organised event to see whose system was most popular.

William Hylton

Using the knowledge he learned as an electrician, William built his own sound system in 1964 so he could play at parties. A hall in Chandos Street, Slough was one of his favourite venues, he remembered that it cost two shillings and sixpence to enter and half a crown for curried goat and drinks. His set was called V-Rocket and he sought out the latest records playing ska, bluebeat, reggae and calypso music for audiences where West Indian and English people mixed.

After he had a family he often took them with his sound system to play at parties, even places as far afield as the Isle of Wight, The Netherlands and Belgium.

Participating in the post-war rebuilding was not limited to labour, as Harry Goulbourne (2018) noted: "the Caribbean presence and participation are particularly strong in the fields of sports and music, theatre and literature, language change and common styles of living such as fashions and family types".

In the field of sport, Eustace was a keen cricket player and later became an athletics coach. When he came to England he played for Slough West Indian Cricket Club, one of the best teams in the South East at the time. After retiring from the sport he put his energies into coaching athletes, a role he took on after assisting his daughters, Emma and Julie, with their training. He began helping out as his daughters' athletics club and eventually took courses to improve his knowledge and skills. He obtained the necessary licenses to be a UK Athletics Coach and assisted with the training of elite athletes who went on to participate in international sporting events. Eustace coached for almost forty years at Windsor, Slough and Eton Athletic Club motivated by a desire to help the athletes achieve their potential. He enjoyed this role immensely and sought to create a friendly atmosphere of respect in order to lay a strong foundation for young people so they could succeed in their sporting disciplines.

William's second child Mark excelled at running and football at school. In 1996 Mark took part in the Atlanta Olympic Games, winning a silver medal for Great Britain in the 4 x 400 metres. Mark's athletic success led to an invite to Buckingham Palace where the family met Prince Philip, who told William he should be proud of his son.

As the previous chapters have shown, the history of the Caribbean documents that by the twentieth century the people were among the world's first modern, de-tribalised people. In the nineteenth century Chinese and Indian indentured labourers arrived, Lebanese and Syrians escaping Ottoman repression also came to the islands. With so many diverse racial and ethnic backgrounds it was easy to see why some family photographs displayed a kaleidoscopic representation of humanity.

Eustace is aware of the Irish influence on St. Kitts, there is a village called Irish Town west of the capital city Basseterre. Reading up about the town, Eustace believes this is where Irish people had a community in the past. His cousin told Eustace that his great-great-great-grandfather was an Irishman. This inspired Eustace to do some research of his own, he found a Herbert from 1870 and he travelled to St. Nevis in 2012 to look at the records and see if he could trace his family tree.

Eustace's time in Slough has always been very busy helping other people and doing as much as he can to contribute towards the wellbeing of the community. In the 1960s and 1970s he was involved with the Slough Race Community Council. He helped with the formation of Slough West Indian Peoples Enterprise (SWIPE). In 1983 Eustace became a Parish Councillor of Slough Borough Council, getting involved as he wanted to contribute as a resident and a citizen of Slough. He felt that by representing people he could resolve difficulties and the challenges that confronted them. For a period he was also the chairman of Slough West Indian Parents Association when he contributed to helping with their activities.

Bill and Gwen Bramble

For some Caribbean people who came to England the circumstances were forced upon them. Bill and Gwen Bramble came from Montserrat, an island renowned for its natural beauty. But in 1995 the Soufrière Hills volcano became active after a long period of dormancy. Plymouth, the capital city, was destroyed by a thick layer of ash and eruptions continued, making over half the island uninhabitable. Two thirds of the population were evacuated and many came to Britain.

The volcano eruption forced Bill and Gwen to flee their home and left them unable to return as their property was located in the exclusion zone in the south of the island. They knew when they moved to Britain it would be a permanent move. As Montserrat was a British colony they were entitled to move to the United Kingdom as British citizens. They came to Slough in 2001 as Gwen's parents and siblings lived there.

Bill has nothing but good memories of Montserrat, he liked the fact that every morning there seemed to be three minutes of rain. For him the place was wonderful, fruitful and beautiful. For Gwen the beauty of Montserrat was its people, a place where everybody would speak to everyone else, say hello and was very friendly. They had a great social life and particularly enjoyed the music: calypso, soca, reggae and the steel bands. They ran a business owning a shop that sold a variety of things from school textbooks to furniture and clothes. Bill also worked as an accountant.

Before they were forced to leave, they had been to Slough numerous times over the years to visit their family. For Bill it felt like a homecoming as he knew so many people when he arrived. Although it is the greatest change he has experienced in his life, for him it has been a wonderful experience making friends with different people, meeting new neighbours and fitting into a new life with very little problems. He had become accustomed to the smaller world and limitations of Montserrat. But now he is exposed to visiting so many different people, so many different towns and he does not regret leaving when he did. Bill has nothing but praise for the people of Slough. They have never felt homesick in the town, with Gwen's parents living in Slough along with her four brothers, her sister and their families it has been easy for them to fit into their new home.

Montserrat is known as the "The Emerald Isle of the Caribbean" due to its Irish heritage. The Brambles take a keen interest in their history and culture, Bill was friends with Dr. George Irish, an academic authority on the history of the island. The St. Patrick's Day celebrations last much longer in Montserrat, Gwen has fond memories of the week long party and recalls the races that were held, the stalls and many people on the streets enjoying themselves.

In spite of being forced to leave their home country Bill feels that we must recognize that changes will come in life, individually and nationally. And we should all embrace every change in harmony.

Irish migration to Britain

Irish migration to Britain has been ongoing for centuries. In the eighteenth century some 250,000 people left Ireland for a new life in the Americas and Australia. The nineteenth century, and in particular the period of the Great Famine in the 1840s, led to a huge exodus from Ireland. The Free Irish State that was established in 1922 suffered from economic problems leading to another wave of emigration from the 1930s to the 1960s. Many Irish came to work in construction, helping to rebuild post-war Britain. The businessman Sir William McAlpine commented "The contribution of the Irish to the success of this industry has been immeasurable".

Paddy Farlan

Paddy and Philomena Farlan lived in Navan, County Meath before they came to England. They experienced the harsh economic climate as their lives in Ireland were marked by uncertainty over work. There was little work and what jobs there were, were not secure and poorly paid.

Paddy used to work for the Irish Glass Bottle Company in a quarry in County Meath. He worked to excavate the white stones to harden the glass bottles. This work was only available due to supply problems caused by the Second World War, when the war broke out it was difficult to import the stones. As peace and normality eventually returned to Europe, the stones were once more sourced from abroad and the Irish quarry closed down.

Philomena Farlan

Philomena worked in a factory owned by a Scottish firm, making Axminister carpets. She enjoyed the work but lack of demand meant her role was cut down to three days a week. The pay was low, five shillings a week for a full week but this was cut to half a crown when they worked less. The low wages and lack of work led Paddy and Philomena to make the decision to move to England.

By the 1960s Irish migrants had established a well-worn path to England as Brannen, Elliott and Phoenix stated in their 2016 study. Migration was seen as a necessity to become economically self-sufficient. Connections were maintained by letter writing, sending money back home and returning for family holidays. Strong Irish communities were established enabling new arrivals to acclimatise and adapt to their new surroundings.

Martin Conroy

Martin Conroy came to England from a mountainous village in the Maam Valley, Connemara, Ireland. Growing up on a farm his routine involved milking the cattle before going to school and coming home to help manage the animals with his mother and sister. Martin's father was living in Slough at the time and his mother wanted to move away from the damp climate of Ireland as it affected her rheumatoid arthritis. There was very little work in Ireland, Martin's father had to move to England to find work, going backwards and forwards over the years. In 1963 the entire family decided to relocate to England permanently.

Martin remembers a great sense of excitement about coming to England and his first impressions were being overwhelmed by the urban expanse as he had never seen so many towns in his life until he came to Slough. They were made to feel very welcome. There was a huge Irish community and Martin's family was part of it. By the time he arrived with his mother and sister their father was one of the most well-known people in the community playing music and making friends with everyone. Martin found the support of this community made it very easy for him to settle in the new town.

Bartley Coyne

Bartley Coyne's experience echoed that of his friend Martin. Bartley came to Slough in 1970 also from the Maam Valley. Lack of work opportunities prompted him to move to England. Before he came to England he joined the Irish Army in 1965 and was able to take part in the sports he enjoyed. He found this period of his life exciting as he was also posted to Cyprus as part of the Peacekeeping Force when he was in the United Nations.

On his return to Ireland he found opportunities lacking as there were less jobs and money to go around. For a few months he helped his father who was building a house, but soon decided that he needed to move to England in order to find work.

On arrival to England, Bartley lived with the extended family of his future wife Evelyn. It was common for the newly arrived to be helped out by their relatives in this way, assisting them find dwellings and work. He lived in Hillingdon and Southall briefly on arrival. Evelyn found accommodation in Slough and Bartley soon followed.

All of the people we interviewed commented on the Irish community that was in place in Slough. Relatives and friends provided a vital support network, helping to find each other work and accommodation.

Martin stated that there seemed to be thousands of Irish when he arrived in Slough. As a young man he remembers that it was a hive of activity. There were so many more pubs on the High Street with people playing music in all of them. Growing up there was always music in the house, Martin's father played in a band and Slough seemed to be teeming with musicians. There were dances everywhere and Martin went to a fantastic dance hall in Slough High Street called the Carlton when he was old enough.

Tom King

Tom King is the licensee and leaseholder of the Herschel Arms pub, one of the social hubs for the people of Slough. Tom recalled how the premises was used as a support link for the community, although the Irish generation who arrived in the 1960s has dwindled somewhat. There were plenty of job opportunities on the Slough Trading Estate, work was plentiful and it was easy to find places to stay. As well as being entertained, people could go to the Herschel Arms to find employment and accommodation. Word would spread in the pub if someone was in need and the community would do their best to help out.

Bartley shared this experience stating that as well as being a hive of cultural activity the pubs were also great places to find work. All one needed to do was to mention it in conversation and a new job could be found the following day. In marked contrast to Ireland, such was the abundance of jobs in England at that time that it was very easy to find work.

London in the 1970s was buzzing due to its established Irish community according to Bartley and he found himself spending a lot of time in West London. His brother Paddy managed the Halfway House pub in Southall, a traditional Irish pub where the very best musicians played every evening. Bartley was part of that culture, playing and singing his music.

There was a huge vibrant Irish community in Slough and within a few weeks Bartley knew them all. Many people were his age, such as Martin Conroy - who are the best of friends. In this environment Bartley was able to pursue his love of soccer and playing Irish music. He played guitar and soon he got a band going, playing at house parties and he was also asked to perform at weddings. Bartley says the Irish community was fantastic, making Slough a home away from home. Philomena commented that her social life was based around this company, "wherever there was Irish we were there". They always made people welcome, asked them about where they came from and their background - making it very easy to make friends and feel accepted.

Tom's Herschel Arms pub is one of the traditional Irish pubs, but one that has adapted as the 1960s generation has declined and the demographic of Slough changed. The venue still hosts traditional Irish music acts, but Tom is interested in providing a platform for all sorts of other music styles that include jazz, rock and middle of the road music. Tom's philosophy is not to be restrictive and to be open to all sorts of musical styles.

The venue also provides a location where musical tutors can teach pupils. In recent years Tom has started poetry and spoken word nights, which are very popular with the younger generation. Keen to give something back to the community, the staff at The Herschel Arms undertakes charity work in order to help the homeless, people with learning difficulties and young carers. Tom finds this work enormously rewarding.

Tom's interview illustrates that though there were large Irish communities in certain towns they were not in any way restrictive, many who came to England preferred the excitement found in these multi-cultural environments to the rural isolation of Ireland. Paddy stated that he found fewer restrictions in England and much more opportunity, so much so that it cemented his view to stay in the country.

Although Martin misses the natural beauty of Connemara, he found Slough such an inspiring place when he arrived. As he was a teenager when he came to England he mixed with other cultures through school. The first house he lived in was in Chalvey and he remembered the arrival of the first Caribbean people marked a change in the area. Martin embraced this and remarked that he mixed with some "wonderful people from another part of the world" and felt lucky that he got to know about a culture he knew nothing of previously. He also enjoyed playing sports and cricket with the Indian boys he grew up with.

Paddy and Philomena never felt homesick because there was constant work and they felt part of a great Irish community in the Slough. Paddy said work was so plentiful that you could get on your bicycle and go from place to place, find four or five jobs in a day and pick the best one to start at the day after. Philomena expected there to be more work and found her first job at Ideal Capsules, manufacturers of aluminium bottle capsules and bottle capsuling machinery.

Like many Irish who came to England, Bartley worked in building construction doing all types of work. In 1974 he became a shuttering carpenter, specialising in creating formwork or shuttering, which are temporary structures used in the concrete pouring process. This was a trade he carried on until his retirement. Working on the buildings meant that he mixed a lot with other cultures: Polish people

Albanians, Ukrainians, South Africans. Bartley says they all got on very well and didn't have any problems with each other.

As with the Caribbean people who came to Slough, the people who came from Ireland also brought their culture over with them. Though not fully aware of this at the time, looking back Bartley can see that he brought Irish traditions with him. He played Gaelic football and hurling, he sang Irish folk songs bringing a part of where he came from in Ireland over to Slough.

Martin played for a great hurling team called St. Mel's. He also enjoyed playing Gaelic football and soccer. He played for Slough Celtic and was one of the founding members of the club. Martin was involved with the running of the Slough Irish Club that organised music and entertainment for the community. He was part of an amateur dramatics group called SID (Slough Irish Drama) that put on plays for a number of years.

Paddy was also a keen sportsman, in 1949 he played at the Croke Park Stadium, Dublin for County Meath Minors. He played Gaelic football in England until he retired from the sport aged thirty-eight. His proudest moment was when his team St. Mel's won "The Double" in 1954 - the London Championship and the Cup. He also played soccer for Iver Village. Philomena commented that they met lots of Irish people around the Gaelic football team and the hurling team. She was always at the matches to support Paddy and loved the welcoming atmosphere at the games.

All of the people we interviewed were grateful for the opportunities England afforded them and many had words of praise for Slough. Martin met his wife in Slough and feels they have been very lucky to have led a great life in the town. He still regularly goes out on a Thursday night with Bartley Coyne to meet various other people, including Paddy and Philomena, who enjoy singing and playing music at the Herschel Arms.

Tom has always been happy living in Slough and only has good words to say about the town. His daughter grew up in in the town and stayed until she was fourteen years of age. When she moved to Ireland she retained her English passport and Tom takes pride in the fact that his daughter is proud to come from Slough.

Tom hopes he can carry on hosting music at his pub and giving something back into the community. He takes satisfaction in helping the disadvantaged and providing entertainment for the younger generation. He has no family now living in Slough, but considers his staff as part of his family. Tom said that he is proud that there is a great community in Slough, he employs great staff and is looking forward to the future continuing the work he finds rewarding.

CONCLUSIONS

Something very unique happened in the Caribbean, a diverse group of Africans were introduced to a wide variety of Irish and other Europeans. Most of the Europeans who came were from lower classes so brought vernacular styles that were not respected by the social elites who listened to concert hall music. It is not possible to know exactly what the early fusions sounded like, but by the time of the blues and the twentieth century many cycles of musical crossover had occurred and there were so many moments of exchange that it is difficult to track.

As well as migration to the Caribbean, there were waves of Irish immigration into mainland USA from the Caribbean and from Ireland. For four centuries, Africans were transported to the Caribbean and USA, not forgetting that Caribbean-born slaves were moving northward. Sailors and travellers also brought new discoveries back with them so there was a huge and continuous exchange of culture underway in this period.

Cycles of musical reinvention and incorporation have always been occurring. The influence Africa had on European music pre-dates the era of slavery with the introduction of the guitar from North Africa to Iberia in the thirteenth century, by the fifteenth century classical composers wrote pieces for the instrument.

Racial differences continue to be emphasised, today certain styles are labelled "black music" and "white music" distinctions that are especially useful for marketers. But the musical core and the dialogue has been mixed for so long that we have styles of music that have emerged from the Black Atlantic – from the era of slavery the music has involved European styles. From the very beginning the music on the plantations was influencing culture even if people had different levels of access to it.

It is not possible to determine the exact nature of interactions between African and Irish people in the seventeenth century Caribbean, but circumstantial evidence suggests they were working on the plantations together. In two cultures where music played an integral role in society it is likely that Afro-Irish fusion would have occurred. Taking the banjo as an example we can see how the instrument was influenced by African gourds, developed in the Caribbean and went on to become a key feature of Jamaican mento folk music and traditional Irish music. The banjo even found a place in the isolated communities of the Appalachian Mountains where former indentured servants found a home and established new communities.

In the twentieth century the descendants of colonised Caribbean people, former slaves and indentured labourers completed the circle of migration and came to the "Mother Country". Cycles of Irish migration have been ongoing for centuries and the lyrics of traditional Irish music recount tales of emigration and a longing for home.

Although there are few documented examples of cultural crossover between African and Irish people in the seventeenth century, our project has revealed these interactions did occur when Afro-Caribbean and Irish people came to Slough. Initially they sought the familiar community of their own people, but worked alongside each other in the factories and on industrial estate. William Hylton organised sound system music events that were also attended by Irish and British people, curious to hear and experience the unfamiliar sounds from Jamaica. Traditional Irish pubs offered a welcome relief to workers at the end of a hard day, as Tom King recalled his establishment was frequented by Irish people accompanied by their Caribbean colleagues from the Ford factory.

People who found themselves dislocated would have turned to music for solace and to find community. The reason the music that has emerged from these experiences, be it Caribbean or Irish, is so powerful and can move people outside of these cultures is because it speaks of pain, exile and reconstitution; the triumph of creating new types of connections and community. The music carries the history and a lot of this is common history.

APPENDIX

"The Old Plantation" featuring slaves dancing to a banjo and percussion
(image circa late 1700s).

A Tribute To Dani Richardson

I first met Dani as a teen playing the violin with his brother at a community function. The next time I came into contact him again was when he started teaching The Slough All Stars Steelband.

Dani taught music to many, both children and young people, as well as people from the older generation and was happiest when teaching young people, inspiring them to reach their fullest potential. Dani taught music for many years at the Orchard Youth and Community Centre eventually becoming the Music Director for SWIPE. One of his many achievements during this time was to hold steel band taster sessions in eight of the senior schools in Slough; from these sessions a group of thirty young people came together from the steel band group Panaecha, their first performance was held at The West Wing in May 2005 and with Dani residing over them as band leader this was a resounding success.

Dani would spend hours teaching a class, but if there was a child that needed extra help to figure out how to do something or they needed extra tuition to help with music exams, he would happily stay behind to help that child until they were confident in what they were learning. As an accomplished vocalist and composer, he trained several choirs and has left behind many pieces of music which are still enriching the lives of those privileged enough to hear them.

Dani played with several bands singing vocals or accompanying on any instruments as needed, he was also session musician for several acts including the singer Gabrielle. He worked with Orlando Gough who wrote the music for the 2012 London Cultural Olympiad – *Tree of Light*.

Dani was a multi-talented young man who excelled in everything he did, teaching in schools, colleges and after school clubs and taught various instruments to all who wanted to learn at SWIPE (violin, guitar and keyboard) and was music leader both at SWIPE and Raspo in Reading teaching the steelpan, in fact I have not known him to come across any instrument he did not master.

I once asked him how old he was when started to play music, his reply: "I was three and wanted a guitar so my dad got me one for Christmas". While speaking with his family after he passed, his dad then retold the story of a three-year-old Dani who did not stop going on about a guitar. What Dani had failed to tell me was that he insisted on a proper guitar, not a toy. He couldn't manage to put across his body, so he stood it up and played it like a double bass.

His mum told of a five year old Dani who came across a teacher who taught the violin in primary school, there and then Dani decided he had to learn to play the instrument. But he was too young by three years in order to join the class; this did not deter Dani who pestered the teacher every day to join the class that the teacher eventually had to ask his mum to explain he was too young to learn. Instead of giving up he upped the amount of time he visited the teacher, who in the end had to get permission from his parents for him to join the class three years early.

There are many anecdotes regarding Dani, whether it was watching him patiently teaching a child to play an instrument or a piece of music, giving vocal training to a child or adult, helping others to realise their dreams, or simply just rolling around the floor letting off steam with youngsters showing them Aikido marital art. It would be done with the biggest smile because he enjoyed bringing happiness to enrich others' lives.

Over the years Dani has been described as "a bright light in this world" and "Most humble and talented to be in touch with".

Dani has left behind a wonderful rich musical legacy for all to enjoy which will never be forgotten. Anyone who has ever been in touch or encountered this young man has always come away feeling more positive.

Our community will certainly be a poorer place without him in it.

Clo Jeffrey

Visit To The International Slavery Museum

On 28 May 2019 SWIPE accompanied young people from Slough on a visit to Liverpool and The International Slavery Museum. The purpose of this day was to understand the nature of slavery and the experiences of those who were enslaved and those who were slave-owners. Before visiting the museum a seminar was held in order to discuss the topics researched on the project and to discover what the young people knew about the issues around slavery.

I learned that both African and Irish people were transported to the Caribbean, though some Irish later prospered and became slave owners. One story that made an impression on me was that of a slave who made an escape during the night and travelled forty-three miles before he was captured. He was brutally beaten until his flesh was exposed - pouring out with blood, then dragged all the way back to the camp and paraded as an example to warn other slaves. This whole experience has been an incredible learning and eye opening journey. I'm so very happy I had this opportunity, for this I am very thankful to everyone who made this happen and everyone who joined with the project.

Charles

I enhanced my knowledge on this visit, learning how slavery affected Africans and also Irish people. Forcibly transported to the Caribbean, these two different ethnicities and cultures came together with music and dance. The suffering they endured was transformed, incorporated into songs of hope and celebratory dances. Popular musicians such as Bob Marley and Ray Charles acknowledged the roots of their music which can be traced back to this period. My hope is that we may be able to conquer modern slavery with hope and "Ubuntu" togetherness.

Yvonne

I learned that Liverpool played a part in slavery, becoming a major port from which ships sailed to Africa in the 1760s to the 1770s. My trip to the national slave museum gave me an insight into a lot of things that happened that I wasn't aware of. I enjoyed researching and sharing our opinions on slavery.

Renae

The experience shed light on the worldwide impact that slavery had. Slavery still exists in some forms today; some examples are sex trafficking and domestic labourers who can suffer abuse. In order for slavery to exist and function, one group of people must feel that they are superior to another - oppressing those they feel are inferior. This can be due to factors such as race, age, ethnicity or religion.

Joy

I learned that there were a lot of people that tried to help stop slavery and people who later fought for the rights of black people, for example Martin Luther King and Rosa Parks. This was in the face of violent opposition from groups such as the Ku Klux Klan. I also learned that the wealth of countries such as Britain, Spain and Portugal was built on trading goods that were harvested by slave labourers.

Natalie

Video And Website

A video and website accompany this book as the other elements of this project.

The video is comprised of interviews with the academics and the people from Slough in order to give an overview of some of the topics discussed in this book.

The website contains all the work on this project, video clips and links to resources for more information. The website address is: www.afroirishlinks.com

Bibliography and Recommended Reading

Books

Barrett Sr., L.E. (1976) *The Sun and the Drum, African Roots in Jamaican Folk Tradition*. Kingston, Jamaica: Sangster's Book Stores in association with Heinemann.

Barrett Sr., L.E. (1997) *The Rastafarians*. Boston: Beacon Press.

Barrow, S., Dalton, P. (1997) *Reggae: The Rough Guide*. London: Rough Guides Ltd.

Bastide, R. (1972) *African Civilization in the New World*. New York: Harper Torch Books.

Bebey, F. (1969, 1975) *African Music, A People's Art*. Brooklyn: Lawrence Hill Books.

Best, C. (1999) *Barbadian Popular Music and the Politics of Caribbean Culture*. Rochester, VT: Schenkman Books.

Brailoiu, C. (1984, edited and translated by A.L. Lloyd) *Problems of Ethnomusicology*. Cambridge: University Press.

Carey, B. (1997) *The Maroon story: The authentic and original history of the Maroons in the history of Jamaica, 1490–1880*. Gordon Town, Jamaica: Agouti Press.

Cassidy, F. G., Le Page, R. B. (1980) *Dictionary of Jamaican English*. Cambridge: Cambridge University Press.

Clarke, P. B. (1986) *Black Paradise: The Rastafarian Movement*. Wellingborough: The Aquarian Press.

Craton, M. (1982). *Testing the Chains: Resistance to Slavery in the British West Indies*. New York: Cornell University Press.

Donnell, A., McGarrity, M., O'Callaghan, E. (2015) *Caribbean Irish Connections: Interdisciplinary Perspectives.* Kingston, Jamaica: University of the West Indies Press.

Dubois, L. (2016) *The Banjo: America's African Instrument.* Cambridge: Harvard University Press.

Dunn, R.S. (1973) *Sugar and Slaves 1624-1713.* London: Jonathan Cape.

Epstein, D. (2003) *Sinful Tunes and Spirituals: Black Folk Music to the Civil War.* Champaign: University of Illinois Press

Holt, T. C. (1992) *The Problem of Freedom: Race, Labor, and Politics in Jamaica and Britain, 1832-1938.* Baltimore: Johns Hopkins University Press.

Ignatiev, N. (1995) *How the Irish Became White.* New York: Routledge Press.

Kurlansky, M. (1992) *A Continent of Islands: Searching for the Caribbean Destiny.* Boston: Da Capo Press.

Manuel, P., Bilby, K., Largey, M. (1995) *Caribbean Currents: Caribbean Music from Rumba to Reggae.* Philadelphia: Temple University Press.

Merriam, A.P. (1964) *The Anthropology of Music.* Chicago: Northwestern University Press.

Olsen, D. E., Sheehy, D.E. (2000, eds.) *The Garland Handbook of Latin American Music.* New York: Garland Publishing.

Philpott, S. B. (1973) *West Indian Migration: The Montserrat Case.* London: Athlone Press.

Puckrein, G.A. (1984) *Little England: Plantation Society and Anglo-Barbadian Politics 1627–1700*. New York: New York University Press.

Rath, R. C. (2003) *How Early America Sounded*. New York: Cornell University Press.

Rattray, R.S. (1954) *Religion and Art in Ashanti*. London: Oxford University Press, Second Impression.

Roberts, J.S. (1972) *Black Music of Two Worlds*. New York: Original Music.

Saakana, S.A. (1980) *Jah music: the evolution of the popular Jamaican song*. London: Heinemann Educational.

Schlesinger, P. (1991) *Media, State and Nation: Political Violence and Collective Identities*. London: Sage Publications.

Shaw, J. (2013) *Everyday Life in the Early English Caribbean. Irish, Africans, and the Construction of Difference*. Athens, Georgia: University of Georgia Press.

Smith, A D. (1991) *National Identity: Ethno nationalism in Comparative Perspective*. Reno, NV: University of Nevada Press.

Stewart, G. (2000) *Rumba on the River, a history of the popular music of the two Congos*. London: Verso.

Stoddard E. (2012) *Positioning Gender and Race in (Post)colonial Plantation Space: Connecting Ireland and the Caribbean*. New York: Palgrave Macmillan US.

Walvin, J. (1994) *Black Ivory: A History of British Slavery*. Washington, D.C: Howard University Press.

Winans, R. (2018, ed.) *Banjo Roots and Branches*. Urbana: University of Illinois Press.

Articles

Beckles, H. (1990) "A 'riotous and unruly lot': Irish Indentured Servants and Freemen in the English West Indies, 1644-1713" in *The William and Mary Quarterly* Vol. 47, No. 4, pp. 503-522.

Bilby, K. (1992) liner notes in *Drums of Defiance: Maroon Music from the Earliest Free Black Communities of Jamaica*. Washington, D.C.: Smithsonian/Folkways Recordings.

Bilby, K. (2001) "Maroon Autonomy In Jamaica" in *Cultural Survival Quarterly Magazine*. Available at: https://www.culturalsurvival.org/publications/cultural-survival-quarterly/maroon-autonomy-jamaica

Bilby, K. (2008) "A Caribbean Musical Enigma: Barbados" in *Caribbean Studies*, Vol. 36, No. 2, pp. 236-240.

Brannen, J., Elliott, H., Phoenix, A. (2016) "Narratives of success among Irish and African Caribbean migrants" in *Ethnic and Racial Studies*, 39:10, 1755-1772, DOI: 10.1080/01419870.2015.1124125

Burrowes, M. (2005) "The Cloaking of a Heritage: The Barbados Landship" in Heuman, G. and Trotman, D. V. (eds.) *Contesting Freedom: Control and Resistance in the Post-Emancipation Caribbean*. Oxford: Macmillan pp. 215-234.

Cooper, C. J. (2007) "Reggae" in *Encyclopaedia Britannica*. Chicago: Encyclopaedia Britannica, Inc.

Emmick, M. S. (1995) "Scottish and Irish Elements of Appalachian Fiddle Music" in *Undergraduate Honors Thesis Collection*, 21. Available at: https://digitalcommons.butler.edu/ugtheses/21

Fergus (2016) "The Irish Banjo" in *The Irish Place*. Available at: https://www.theirishplace.com/traditional-irish-music/the-irish-banjo/

Fields, L. (2011) "4-string Banjo in Jamaican Mento Music" in *Banjo Hangout*. Available at: https://www.banjohangout.org/blog/24475

Foner, N. (2008) "Gender and Migration: West Indians in Comparative Perspective" in *Wiley Online Library*. Available at: https://onlinelibrary.wiley.com/doi/pdf/10.1111/j.1468-2435.2008.00480.x

Gangelhoff, C. (2013) "Art-Music by Caribbean Composers" in *At The Barbados Archives*. Heritage: Art Music by Bajan Composers. Available at: https://atthebarbadosarchives.wordpress.com/2013/02/21/heritage-art-music-by-bajan-composers/

Garnice, M. (2018) "What is Mento Music?" in *Mento Music*. Available at: http://www.mentomusic.com/WhatIsMento.htm

Goulbourne, H. (2018) "Windrush and the making of post-imperial Britain" in *British Library*. Available at: https://www.bl.uk/windrush/articles/windrush-and-the-making-of-post-imperial-britain

Grace, J. (n.d.) "Do You Remember the Days of Slavery? A Study of the Oppression of the Jamaican Working Class 1834-1942" in *The Dread Library*. Available at: https://debate.uvm.edu/dreadlibrary/grace.html

"History Notes: Information on Jamaica's Culture and Heritage" in *The National Library of Jamaica*. Available at: https://nlj.gov.jm/history-notes-jamaica/

Hogan, L., McAtackney, L., Reilly, M. C. (2016) "The Irish in the Anglo-Caribbean: servants or slaves?" in *History Ireland*. Published in 18th-19th Century Social Perspectives, Issue 2, Vol. 24. Available at: https://www.historyireland.com/18th-19th-century-history/18th-19th-century-social-perspectives/the-irish-in-the-anglo-caribbean-servants-or-slaves/

Kauppila, P. (2006) "From Memphis to Kingston: An Investigation into the Origin of Jamaican Ska" in *Social and Economic Studies*, Vol. 55, No. 1-2, pp. 75-91. Available at: https://openmusiclibrary.org/article/64600/

"Jamaica's Heritage in Music" (2018) in *The Jamaica Information Service*. Available at: https://jis.gov.jm/information/jamaicas-heritage-dance-music/jamaicas-heritage-music/

"Jamaica's Heritage in Dance" (2018) in *The Jamaica Information Service*. Available at: https://jis.gov.jm/information/jamaicas-heritage-dance-music/jamaicas-heritage-dance/

Lingold, M.C. (2017) "Peculiar Animations: Listening to Afro-Atlantic Music in Caribbean Travel Narratives" in *Early American Literature* 52(3), 623-650. doi:10.1353/eal.2017.0052.

Marcus, T. (n.d.) "Harmony and Howling - African and European Roots of Jamaican Music" in *The Dread Library*. Available at: https://debate.uvm.edu/dreadlibrary/marcus.html

"Maroon Expressive Culture - Music, Dance, and Songs" (2016) in *Jamaican Maroons*. Available at: http://www.grannynannymaroons.com/maroon-expressive-culture-music-dance-and-songs/

Marshall, T. G., Watson, E. F. (2004) "Barbados" in *Music in Latin America and The Caribbean*, Vol 2. Austin: University of Texas Press. pp. 345–357.

McClatchy, D. (2000) "Appalachian Traditional Music - A Short History" in *Musical Traditions Internet Magazine*. Available at: http://www.mustrad.org.uk/articles/appalach.htm

McDowell, L. (2018) "How Caribbean migrants helped to rebuild Britain" in *British Library*. Available at: https://www.bl.uk/windrush/articles/how-caribbean-migrants-rebuilt-britain

"Mento purely home-grown" in *Jamaica Gleaner*. Published: 6 July 2014. Available at: http://jamaica-gleaner.com/gleaner/20140706/ent/ent6.html

Meredith, S. (2004) "Barbadian Tuk Music – A Fusion of Musical Cultures" in Randall, A. (ed.) *Music, Power and Politics*. Oxford: Routledge.

Merriam, A.P. (1960) "Ethnomusicology: Discussion and Definition of the Field". Published by: University of Illinois Press on behalf of Society for *Ethnomusicology*. DOI: 10.2307/924498. Available at: https://www.jstor.org/stable/924498

Messenger, J.C. (1975) "Montserrat: The Most Distinctively Irish Settlement in the New World" in *Ethnicity* 2: pp. 281–303.

Millington, J. (1999) "Barbados" in *Garland Encyclopaedia of World Music*, Vol. 2. Oxford: Routledge. pp. 813–821.

Moloney, M. (1986) "The Banjo - A Short History" in O'Connor, G., McNevin, D. *50 Solos for Irish Tenor Banjo*. Dublin: Walton's. Available from *The Standing Stones*: http://www.standingstones.com/banjo.html

Nettl, B. (1985) "The Concept of Preservation in Ethnomusicology" in Jackson, I. V. (ed.) *More Than Drumming, Essays on African and Afro-Latin American Music and Musicians* 19:3. Westport, CT: Greenwood Press.

Ó Siochrú, M. (2008) "'Shipped for the Barbadoes': Cromwell and Irish migration to the Caribbean'" in *History Ireland*. Published in Confederate War and Cromwell, Early Modern History (1500–1700), Issue 4, Vol. 16. Available at: https://www.historyireland.com/early-modern-history-1500-1700/shipped-for-the-barbadoes-cromwell-and-irish-migration-to-the-caribbean/

Parker, J. (1972) "Sugar and Slaves: The Rise of the Planter Class in the English West Indies, 1624–1713" in *History: Reviews of New Books*, 1:1, 4, DOI: 10.1080/03612759.1972.9954929.

Rodgers, N. (2017) "The Irish in the Caribbean 1641-1837: An Overview" in *Irish Migration Studies in Latin America*. Available at: https://www.irlandeses.org/0711_145to155.pdf

Scully, M. (2015) "'Emigrants in the traditional sense?' – Irishness in England, contemporary migration, and collective memory of the 1950s" in *Irish Journal of Sociology*. Available at: https://journals.sagepub.com/doi/abs/10.7227/IJS.23.2.9

Smith M.G., Augier, R., Nettleford, R. (1960) "The Ras Tafari Movement in Kingston, Jamaica" (Institute of Social and Economic Research, University College of the West Indies) in *Caribbean Quarterly* Vol. 13, No. 3, pp. 3–29; and Vol. 13, No. 4, pp. 3–14.

Sterling, M. (2005) Review of "Wake the Town and Tell the People: Dancehall Culture in Jamaica" by Stolzoff, N. *Canadian Journal of Latin American and Caribbean Studies / Revue canadienne des études latino-américaines et caraïbes*. Vol. 30, No. 59, pp. 200-202. Available at: http://www.jstor.org/stable/41800256

Stowell, C. R. (2000) "Retention and Preservation of African Roots in Jamaican Folk Music" In *The Dread Library*. Available at: https://debate.uvm.edu/dreadlibrary/stowell.html

Waterman, C.A. (1991) "The Uneven Development of Africanist Ethnomusicology: Three Issues and a Critique" in Nettl, B., Bohlman, P.V. (eds.) *Comparative Musicology and Anthropology of Music*. Chicago: University of Chicago Press. pp. 169-186.

Williams, A.R. (1997) "Under the Volcano: Montserrat" in *National Geographic* 192 (1). pp. 58–75.

Websites

Musical Passages
www.musicalpassage.org
This website offers an interpretation of the music recorded in Hans Sloane's *Voyage to the Islands of Madera, Barbados, Nieves, S. Christophers and Jamaica* written in 1707. On a single page within this book is the notation of music performed at a gathering of black musicians in Jamaica. A collaborative project by Laurent Dubois, David Garner, and Mary Caton Lingold.

The Dread Library
https://debate.uvm.edu/dreadlibrary/dreadlibrary.html
A selection of essays on reggae music and its various social, political, and religious manifestations.

Images

Images courtesy of The British Library and Wiki Commons Library.

Afro-Irish Links Project Team

Hilton Callaghan: Team Advisor

Jennifer Callaghan: Research

Michael Callaghan: Research

Paul Crooks: Research

Frank Doherty: Project Leader, Research

Clo Jeffrey: Administration and Team Leader

Robert Martin Kelly: Film Production and Research

Slough West Indian Peoples Enterprise (SWIPE)

Registered Charity: 1107921.

SWIPE was formed in 1997 to help further the education and training of children and young people at risk of being excluded from school. It also offers single parent families and over forty's assistance in the creation of employment opportunities.

SWIPE develops and produces high impact community projects for the people of Slough, with effective outputs in a wide variety of activities, including but not exclusively music tuition, as well as dance, music, sports, film, community cohesion and heritage we also continue supporting the celebratory activities of other local charities by offering our support to them with advice, event management and provision of music.

SWIPE's recent offer has included music education and performance opportunities, alongside artist development, rehearsal space and recording opportunities. We have collaborated on film soundtracks and additional sound recording in film with partners working on films for the BBC, Channel 4 and others.

SWIPE is a founder member and one of the lead organisations of Youth Engagement Slough consortium who work to provide regular activities for young people across the whole borough.

SWIPE continues to seek funds and create opportunities wherever possible to continue to work and foster community cohesion for the benefit of the people of Slough.

SWIPE is recognised and celebrated for its work in forming the first volunteer police cadet unit in the Thames Valley, in recognition of this Slough Police Cadets have a gold pin with the word SWIPE as part of their uniform.

SWIPE's new building at the Jubilee River in Slough, has now become successful with its new timetable and offer to the community of regular activities such as paddle boarding, rowing and kayaking.

The Riverside Centre also provides activities for local schools to become involved in water sports on this underused man-made river in the borough.

SWIPE held a successful Riverside festival bringing together Music Art and sport at the river, we intend to continue developing an artistic offer at the river as well as our sports provision.

We are involved in community clean ups on the river with our partners Thames21 and continue to provide volunteering opportunities for other organisations and companies, such as Slough Estates Group (Segro), Mars, Google, Urenco and others who invest time, money and resources in the development of the centre, as well as the maintenance of the river and its surrounding areas.

SWIPE provides opportunity for the Caribbean community to preserve its Heritage and seek to gain funding for this purpose.

SWIPE has continued to be seen as an innovative organisation producing high quality projects and has yet again received an award for its work, this time the 2016 Thames Heritage Award from The River Thames Society to compliment the previous awards: Get Berkshire Active Youth Engagement Project of the Year 2015; Winner of Sportivate project of the year South East 2016; National winner of Sport England Sportivate Bronze Award 2016; and Slough Business Community Partnership's Project of the year 2016 in recognition of the work and commitment in establishing the Jubilee Riverside Centre as an excellent facility for local people